# Redemption

A Personal Journey of Healing Found in a
Journey Through the Book of Ruth

Heidi Rei

# dedication

**To my Daughters,**

**Hillary Brooke and Hannah Corinne** :

*It was your faces that I fixed my eyes on while walking out my own journey of Redemption.*

*You will never know the courage you gave me to keep walking on the days that I wanted to quit. Your love, prayers, and support have meant the world to me.*

*I am so grateful that you are my daughters.*

*I love you, and I am so proud of the young women you both have become!*

Mom

#  forward

The *Heidi Reiszner* I know has always been an avid student of God's word. Her studies, along with a unique skill set of communicating biblical principles in a very practical way, are like keys used to unlock the holed places of so many lives! I have witnessed it over and over again as Heidi has shared not just information, but also personal revelation mixed with humor and vulnerability as she has taught life changing biblical truths. I count it an honor to forward the first of many Heidi Reiszner's books...this girl is a deep well! Most impressive, however, is the wife, mother, sister, and loyal friend she is. One of my greatest privileges has been to have both a front row seat as well as a behind the scenes perspective into Heidi's mountain top and valley moments. What a genuine gift from God that Heidi is to me and so many who have the joy of calling her friend.

A final note: As I was reading this AMAZING book, I was grateful for the reminder that my pain is not futile. It has a future! Thank you my friend.

Graciously,

*Michelle Aranza*

# table of contents

# discussion questions

The discussion questions that I've included at the end of each chapter are as important as the chapter itself. It is within these questions that real, practical steps will become the guidance you need to experience the healing and wholeness that God desires for you.

Please don't skip these sections. Take the time to stop, pause, and ponder at the end of each chapter to hear and receive all that God desires to speak to your heart. It is vital in your journey to complete healing.

These questions are formatted to be used in a small group setting but can also be used as a guideline for your personal study and journaling.

I encourage you to gather a group of your girlfriends, co-workers, neighbors, or family members to read through this book together and use these questions as a springboard into further discussion, accountability, and prayer points.

If you choose to read this book alone, I encourage you to use these questions to further assist in your healing process. Read through these questions as you complete each chapter, then pause, pull out your Bible, journal, and write out your thoughts, prayers, and even pains as you allow the Holy Spirit to touch the most tender places of your heart.

You may even choose to read the book through in its entirety first, and then go back chapter-by-chapter and journal through the discussion questions.

Regardless of how you choose to implement these questions, whether in a small group format, or alone with only you and God, my purpose in writing them is to give you some practical applications in walking out the message of this book. My prayer for you is that as you discuss or journal through the questions, the healing process of your heart will begin.

# *introduction*

*I've* always loved the word of God. Growing up in church, the love for God's Word has been in my heart since childhood. I've read it, memorized it, meditated on it, and found direction, guidance, strength, comfort, and peace in its pages. His words have never failed me and have never ceased to amaze me. By knowing God's words, you know His heart. That is how I read the Bible. Not to just get through my reading plan or to check off another chapter, but to know God - to really know Him, His character, and His heart.

It was not surprising that the Bible was the place God led me as my extended family and I faced a time of great tragedy and loss. My husband and I were living and pastoring a church in Houston, Texas in the year 2000 when I received a phone call that my uncle (who was more like an older brother to me) and cousin had been tragically killed in a motorcycle accident. My hometown was several hours away, but I immediately jumped in my car and headed home to my family. We faced sorrow, brokenness, and heartache together. It was a senseless accident, no fault of my uncle or cousin. An innocent motorcycle ride turned fatal because of someone else's careless driving.

After the funeral, upon returning to my own family and home and while we were still mourning our loss, God asked something of me. He placed on my heart the book of Ruth. He asked me to read it. To study it. To know it. At that time, I had read through the Bible every year since I was a teenager, and I continue to do so. I had already read the book of Ruth many times and had a deep love and appreciation for the book. As an adult, I had even taught many times from the book of Ruth. This time was to be different. This time was to be divine. It was to be healing. It was to be prophetic. It was to paint a picture of my own life journey and give an explanation to so many questions I had in my mind. Questions of family, of loss, of heartache, of pain, and of brokenness. This time was to also paint a beautiful picture of redemption and grace and hope. Because, you see, my extended family had been broken, suffered much relational loss, and walked a life-long journey of dysfunction, heartache, and pain long before the accident with my uncle and cousin ever happened. All the tragedy did was expose the brokenness that was already there.

What I did not know then, but I know now, was that God was going to use the book of Ruth to bring healing and wholeness to the fragmented pieces of my own heart and soul.

For over sixteen years, I've done exactly that. I've read it, studied it, and know it. I've read the book of Ruth inside and out. I've studied it in every version possible. I've read every commentary ever written on it. I've spoken more messages out of the book of Ruth than I can count. I've written and taught so many bible studies over the years from this book that I don't even need my notes anymore. The book of Ruth is IN me and ON me and has brought great healing to my once very broken life. In many ways, I've placed my own life in the book of Ruth and walked through its pages as if I were one of its characters.

The book of Ruth is only four chapters long, but much is packed into those chapters. It's a story of a family: an ordinary family that walked through hardship and suffering, pain and loss, then divinely journeyed into purpose and destiny, redemption and grace.

There was nothing special about this family. This family did not have a priest, king, or prophet in it. At least, not yet. It's the story of a husband and wife and their two sons who married foreign girls. It is the story of tragedy and heartache. A story of a family losing their way and losing one another - not too different from our families today. Nothing extra special about them. They were just a family making tough decisions in the midst of tough times. They were a family that was broken, lost, and looking for a way back to what used to be or back to what was supposed to be.

The book of Ruth is a story of family and a story of relationships. It is a story that gives all families hope, no matter how far its members have strayed away or how broken they have become.

This book you hold in your hands is simply MY journey of family. It is my story, my perspective, my mistakes, and the personal life lessons that God has taught me along the way. It is a conversation that I have had with countless women for more than twenty-five years. It is those conversations that I have now written into words for many more women to be a part of.

Join me, will you, as we walk through the pages of this most special book? If you look really closely, I have a feeling you will find yourself within the pages of this story too.

.

# The Story of A Family

*Ruth 1:1*
*"In the days when the judges ruled..."*

Remember when you were a little girl and you played "make-believe" with your friends? With all the electronic gadgets available today, I don't know if children even have the opportunity to play "make-believe", but I still remember the game and the fun we would have. I was always, and I do mean always, a teacher or a preacher. Every. Single. Time. A loving, wise, well-versed teacher or a fire and brimstone, even at times, a singing preacher leading hymns from the hymn book! I cannot remember playing make-believe and not being one of those two things. I would line up chairs in my bedroom to serve as a classroom or a congregation, depending on what mood I was in. Regardless of which one I went with on a particular day, I always (and again I do mean ALWAYS) had a microphone in my hand, speaking to my classroom or congregation, and I was always (there is that word again) telling my students or parishioners what to do. My classroom or congregation usually consisted of my younger sister, some stuffed animals, and Barbie dolls. My microphone ranged from a hairbrush to the wooden finial taken from the post of my bed. I would be in the front of the chairs, either teaching a classroom lesson, preaching a sermon, or singing a hymn (before I preached my sermon). I was only five or six years old at the time, and looking back over forty years ago, God certainly had a sense of humor…or more importantly, an absolute sense of purpose for my life.

As an adult, I have taught elementary school. I was a children's pastor for over ten years, and eventually, a teacher/preacher of God's Word. (I was never a worship leader, thank God!) Had I known growing up that I would indeed become a teacher/preacher, it would have scared me to death, or maybe it would have even puffed me up with pride. Either way, it's a good thing I didn't know. God's way is usually not to tell us the "rest of the story" because if we knew the whole story and how our lives would turn out ahead of time, we wouldn't need faith: faith to trust that He is with us, faith to understand that His plans are greater than our plans, faith to understand that God does know best for us. That's why our Christian journey is known as a "walk of faith". Without faith it is impossible to know and please Him. (Hebrews 11:6) Faith kicks in when we can't find the answer, see the end, or feel His presence with us. Faith is simply knowing that He walks with us and guides our steps, trusting that we're headed in the right direction.

That same faith is very evident in this family that we will journey with through the book of Ruth. There is no direct mention of God in the book of Ruth. We don't see God showing up on the scene and speaking to this family. We don't see Him perform any miracles, nor do we see this family praying to or calling out to their God. Because of where they lived and the people they belonged to, we can draw an accurate conclusion that this family knew God and loved Him. They were Israelites living in Bethlehem, Judah, and they served the one, true God.

Even though God is not seen or spoken of directly in this book, we see His work indirectly throughout its pages. Just because we can't see Him, doesn't mean He isn't there. He is all over everything that is happening. God is moving, directing, and working throughout this story. He is most certainly there. No doubt about it.

Isn't that the case in our lives as well? There are seasons of our lives when we can recognize the hand of God and sense or feel His presence with us, but there are also times when we wonder where in the world He is. We love God and know Him, but we don't clearly see Him working. We don't tangibly feel His presence or His direction. Make no mistake about it, HE IS THERE. Whether you see Him or not, whether you sense His presence or not, whether you clearly see Him in action or not, HE IS THERE. God is IN and ALL OVER whatever season you are walking through right now. His word promises that He will "never leave us or forsake us" (Hebrews 13:5). That doesn't mean you will always feel God with you or see Him moving in your life. Many times, you will have to simply trust that He's there. Because He is. He's working and moving on your behalf, even when it doesn't feel like it. Hebrews 11:1 (NLT) defines faith as "the confidence that what we hope for will actually happen; it gives us assurance about things we cannot see". The remaining verses in Hebrews 11 speak of what Christians refer to as the "Hall of Faith", the accounts of men and women who were known for their great faith, not because they had always seen God before the fact, but because looking back at their journey, God was very evident and at work in their lives. Through their stories of great faith, we draw strength and encouragement that God is with us and working for us as well.

I cannot tell you how many times over the years I've wondered if God was really with me or if He really cared about what was going on in my life. It felt as if I was alone, navigating through a difficult season, not clearly seeing God's hand in a particular situation. It wasn't until I looked back after that season had passed did I so clearly and lovingly see God graciously and faithfully walking with me, even in times when it didn't feel like He was! I've come to realize that it's always easier to see God looking behind me than it is looking forward. As we walk forward, it takes trust and faith to go and do or obey all that He is asking of us. It's usually not until we've reached our goal or our place of obedience that we can look back and see God in each and every step that we took to get there.

I have a feeling that as Naomi and Ruth looked back over the journey they took, they could wholeheartedly see God in a BIG way! They were walking forward into a new season, a new life, new challenges, and new promises. They were probably just as scared as me, wondering if God was really with them. We have the privilege of knowing the rest of their story. God sees the end of your story too, and He knows how it will turn out. It's going to be good…very good. You have to just keep walking and trusting that He is there with you. I promise, when you look back, you too will see a BIG God, all over and all in your story!

*"In the days when the judges ruled…" Ruth 1:1*

The story of Naomi's family isn't that different from many families today. They were a family just like yours and mine. They found themselves walking through dark, uncertain times just like we do today.

The first phrase of Ruth chapter 1, *"In the days when the judges ruled…"* tells us a great deal about this family and the difficult times they were facing. These were some of the darkest times in the history of Israel. God had delivered the Israelites out of captivity in Egypt, brought them through the wilderness, and led them into the Promised Land (Canaan). You would think that this new generation (the old generation had died) of Israelites would serve God in a wonderful way, but they didn't.

The story of the book of Ruth happened during the time when "the judges ruled", meaning there was no king to rule over its people. The book of Judges tells of a sad departure from God, how people once served the living and true God then turned from Him to idolatry and moral corruption, how they cried out to Him when the enemy oppressed them, and how God raised up judges to deliver and lead them.

Judges 17:6 tells us that *"...everyone did as he saw fit"*. The people had cast off restraint and lived their lives with no conviction or remembrance of all God had delivered them from. Those were dark days for the Israelite people. Those dark days are where the story of Elimelech, Naomi, and their sons begins.

That sounds very familiar to where we are today in our nation, doesn't it? We watch it every night on the news and receive updates every hour on our smartphones. We have become a nation that has cast off all restraint and turned our backs on God. There is no right and wrong, no moral or ethical standards by which to live our lives. Whatever feels good...do it. We are free to say whatever comes to our minds, regardless of the pain it will bring to others, and call it "free speech". We have become a people not concerned with the consequences of our words or actions. **We live for the moment of now and worry about our future later.**

"Everyone did as they saw fit" not only perfectly describes the time in which Naomi and her family lived, but it also perfectly describes the day and age that we live in today. It was a desperate time for Elimelech and Naomi, and it may be a desperate time for your family too.

The American family has come under attack like never before. In fact, the very definition of marriage has been redefined in our nation. Did you ever think we would live to see such a day? Mothers and fathers are walking out of marriages because it's just too hard to make it work, and the world promises a much better life for them. Children are suffering at a level unlike anything we've ever seen in our lifetimes. Good is being called evil, and evil is being called good (Isaiah 5:20).

The attack on our families shouldn't come as a surprise to us though. From the beginning of time, Satan's strategy has been to destroy the family, whether it be with Adam and Eve, Cain and Abel, Joseph and his brothers, or David and his children. The list goes on and on. The family has always been a target for the enemy. Once the family becomes broken, the brokenness trickles down to every other area in society - the church, the school, the government, etc. **God created the family before He created the church. He knows the authority, influence, and purpose that a strong, healthy family can have in this fallen world, but so does the enemy. That is the reason why the attack on the family unit is so great.**

In the upcoming chapters we will see that Elimelech made a decision for his family out of the chaos of their season that would affect his family deeply. We would be wise to learn from his decision in the most uncertain of times.

# CHAPTER 1

*discussion questions*

**1.** What was that make-believe character you played as a child? Why do you think you chose that particular character, role, or occupation to play?

**2.** Does that make-believe character have any resemblance to what you are doing as an adult? Why or why not?

**3.** Describe a season in your life when you felt it was hard to see God at work, but looking back, you can now see Him clearly intervening during that season.

**4.** Share your biggest "walk of faith" season to date. What are some of the lessons you learned during that time in your life?

**5.** In your opinion, what has been the biggest factor in the decline of the American family in the past ten years? The past 20 years?

**6.** Naomi and her family lived during a time in which "everyone did as they saw fit". Describe, through your own perspective and experiences, how that same phrase is so true for us today.

# Living in the Land of Famine

*Ruth 1:1-2*

*"There was a famine in the land. So a man from Bethlehem
in Judah, together with his wife and two sons, went to live
for a while in the country of Moab. The man's name was
Elimelech, his wife's name was Naomi, and the names of
his two sons were Mahlon and Kilion. They were Ephra-
thites from Bethlehem, Judah. And they went to Moab and
lived there."*

*I*n over twenty-seven years of marriage, my husband and
I have lived in many different places. From the inner-cities to small
towns and everywhere in between. Ranging from an old, dilapidat-
ed garage apartment that also served as church nursery classrooms
(true story ☺), to multiple rent houses that housed multiple rodents,
to living with our three small children in a small cabin on our church
property, to finally owning our own home. We have lived in pretty

much every different kind of house you can think of, but there is one place we've never lived…the desert. While we have visited an actual desert, we have never set up camp there. While deserts do have their own unique beauty, I have never personally desired to live there, especially in the deserts of the Middle East. It has never been on our list of top ten places to live. However, that is exactly where Elimelech and his family ended up. They moved to a forbidden country with their two sons and found themselves in the biggest desert season of their lives. Deserts are hot, lonely, and sandy with very little vegetation (fruit) of any kind. Consequently, desert seasons in our spiritual lives can feel exactly the same way. In spiritual seasons of famine, it seems that God is far away. His voice is not easily heard, and bearing fruit in your life seems next to impossible as all "life" seems to be drained from your dry, barren squelched heart. But even more painful, is the fact that it seems as if you're the only person experiencing the famine. You find yourself in a season all alone, or at least it feels that way. It's certainly not a season you would choose, and it is definitely not a place you would want to live. Desolate countries aren't the first place you think of to move with your family. Elimelech did, and the desolate country and desert season did not serve him or his family well. Let's first back up and look at how this move came about.

Ruth 1:1 tells us that Elimelech moved his family to the country of Moab because there was a famine in Bethlehem. A famine, where food and water are scarce, caused Elimelech to pack up his family and move to a different country in hopes of a better life. By just reading that one verse, it doesn't sound too harmful. It actually sounds pretty reasonable until you understand the background of Bethlehem in contrast to the background of Moab. Bethlehem, which means the "house of bread", and Judah, which means "praise", was a rich agricultural area. Biblical names were very significant and held a prophetic meaning to those it was placed upon. Bethlehem sounds like a wonderful place to live, doesn't it?

This family lived in the "house of bread (provision)" and "praise," but, because of a famine, decided to leave and move to the country of Moab. This is one of thirteen famines mentioned in the Bible. Every time a famine is spoken of in Scripture, it usually signifies a judgment from God as a result of the people's disobedience. Apparently, Elimelech didn't believe that God could take care of him and his family in the "house of bread and praise" during the famine, so he moved them to Moab.

The country of Moab was one of the nations that oppressed Israel during the period of the judges (Judges 3:12), and there was much hostility between the two nations. Psalms 108:9 describes Moab as "my wash pot" or "wash basin" (a bucket where one would wash their feet). The Message version even says, "Moab is my scrub bucket...I mop the floors with Moab." Moab was a country created out of an incestuous relationship (Genesis 19:36-37) whose people created a country of outcast people serving false and idolatrous gods.

Why in the world would Elimelech move his family to such a place? Knowing the hostility between the two nations and their vastly differing views of who the One, True God was, it's almost as if Elimelech was walking away from everything he had known and believed.

His decision doesn't make any sense to us. It seems absurd. Both in Biblical times as well as today, famines can cause people to do crazy things. The distance between Bethlehem and Moab was a seven to ten day journey. There was one week's distance between the land of provision and praise to the land of the wash pot.

**One land had a famine; the other land was the famine.**

It's funny what people will do during a famine season in their lives. The senseless decisions people have made in those desert seasons are difficult to understand. Many have broken my heart. As a pastor I have seen men walking out on their wives and children to begin a new life with a new, younger wife. Women are walking out on their husbands and children to live the single life they say they have always wanted. Sports cars are bought and cosmetic surgeries are scheduled with the hopes of finding a better "land" in which to live. During financial famines, I've seen sensible adults cast off all restraint and get in debt over their heads just because they're tired of living within their means. They became weary in trusting God to meet all of their needs.

A dry, lonely famine season can cause people to do crazy things. Just look at Elimelech or even at your own season of famine. Famine seasons make us want to run far away - away from everybody and everything. In reality, the opposite is true. It is in our seasons of famine that it becomes vital for us to stay close to the people that God has divinely placed in our lives - people that know and love us and can see clearly on our behalf in times when we cannot.

In a famine season, people do one of two things: they run away from God (like Elimelech) or they run to God (as we shall soon see in Ruth). If we will choose to run to God in those difficult seasons, there will be valuable lessons to be learned about God, His character, and His ways that will give us great wisdom for other difficult seasons we will walk through in the future.

Over my lifetime, I've walked through some terribly difficult famine seasons. I am most certain there will be other desert seasons in which to walk, but I've learned some valuable lessons along the way in how to navigate these most trying seasons:

### 1) **Don't allow a season of famine to drive you away from the place where God has you.**

Just because you've entered into a famine season doesn't mean you're in the wrong place or with the wrong people. It just means God may not seem as evident as He once was. He's still with you but not as clearly as you would like.

Moab always looks good in a season of famine! In fact, ANY place other than your season of famine looks goods to you. Whether it be an old boyfriend, a past lifestyle, a new husband, or a different city in which to live, any new change always looks better than it really is when you're walking through a difficult season.

Whether it be in church life, married life, career life, or family life, famine seasons will come. Do not jump ship during difficult times or seasons. Stay true to where and whom God has placed you with. Do not fall into the temptation of leaving a place or a people that God has connected you with just because dry seasons may come. Famine seasons will come in all of our lives, but it is only a season. It will pass. Just stay faithful where you are, trusting God that a new season is coming!

### 2) Never make a major decision when you're walking through a dry, famine season.

You cannot trust your own judgment or decision making in a season of famine. Your emotions will be telling you one thing while your heart may be saying something else, and your mind cannot decide which one to listen to! ☺ Wait until the season passes (and it will!), then seek God, His Word, and Godly counsel before making your decision. Proverbs 15:22 tells us that wisdom is found in a multitude of counselors. If your decision is truly of God, it will be confirmed by the peace of God in your heart, in the Word of God, and through the people that He has divinely placed in your life.

I have experienced many times in my life that clarity comes once the fog of the famine season dissipates. I then find myself in a much better frame of mind to seek God, His Word, and Godly counsel in making my decision.

3 ) **There are times when God allows a season of famine to come so that He can move us to a divine place.**

This wasn't the case with Elimelech, but it was the case with a prophet named Elijah. In I Kings 17:1, God tells Elijah, *"there will be neither dew nor rain in the next few years except at my word."* God then speaks direction to Elijah, leads him to a brook from which he will drink, and commands the ravens to feed him.

But in verse 7 it says, *"Some time later the BROOK DRIED UP because there had been no rain in the land."* Of course the brook dried up! God had spoken there would be no rain. The very thing God had provided as nourishment and hydration for Elijah was the very thing God caused to dry up. He stopped the rain from coming and replenishing the brook.

Once the brook dried up, the word of the Lord came to Elijah giving him his next step of direction. Verse 8 says, *"Then the word of the Lord came to him (Elijah): Go at once to Zarephath."* Elijah obeyed God and the miracle for the widow of Zarephath happened. After Elijah's obedience, God provided food for him, the widow, and her family. Later in chapter seventeen, God even uses Elijah to raise the widow's son from the dead. The brook drying up is what forced Elijah to get up and move to the next divine place God had for him, and it was God moving him!

These miracles would not have happened had God not caused the

brook to dry up. There will be times in our lives when our place of provision and promise seem to "dry up". It may be the hand of God causing it to dry up to get us to move to the next divine place He has for us.

Sometimes the brook just dries up, and sometimes it is God who is drying it up!

The difference between Elimelech and Elijah was the reason for the famines. The famine God sent to Bethlehem was a punishment to His people who were disobedient. Bethlehem was the place of provision and praise, but a season of famine came so that the people would turn their hearts back to God. In Elijah's case, famine came so that Elijah would get up and go to the place and person where God needed him, the widow of Zarephath and her son. There was a miracle waiting to happen for them, and God intended to use Elijah to perform it. The famine came, (the brook dried up) to get Elijah to move TOWARDS God's plan. Conversely, as famine came to Bethlehem, Elimelech moved AWAY from God's plan.

The choice is always up to us as to which way we will go in a famine. We just have to have the discernment of the Holy Spirit and heart of God to know if it is God who is moving us to a new place He has need of us or if it is our own natural instinct wanting to leave our uncomfortable place of famine.

My pastor often says, "The blessings of God will always follow your obedience." We see this principle played out throughout Scripture, and it's so true. God will always bless our steps of obedience, maybe not immediately, but God's blessings will eventually catch up to our acts of obedience. I also know the opposite to be true. God's blessings will not follow our steps of disobedience. We cannot be disobedient to God or His Word and expect blessings to follow us. In fact, it's just the opposite. Consequences and hardships follow our disobedience.

A good parent would never reward or bless their children for acts of disobedience or defiance. They bless and reward their children for acts of obedience, joyfully and rightly so! Our Heavenly Father is the perfect parent Who blesses His children with good gifts, rewards, and blessings for their obedience to Him.

Elimelech and his family found themselves in a literal season of famine that caused him to pack up and move away from God's place of provision and praise. God's blessings did not follow them on their move. What was once a blessed, fruitful life now turned into a dry, famine season that would soon bring great loss and suffering to this family.

There will be times in our lives that we, too, will find ourselves in a famine season simply because God has allowed that season to come to us or possibly because of our own choices and decisions. Perhaps it is by no choice of our own. Maybe life has just led us there.

If you're currently in a famine season in your life and you're not clear as to how you got there, ask yourself these questions:

**Do I have any known sin in my life?**

Sin separates us from God. You will find yourself in a desert season if there is unconfessed sin in your life. However, in 1 John 1:9 it tells us, *"If we confess our sins, He is faithful and just to forgive us of our sins and to cleanse us from all unrighteousness."*

Confess your sins to God. Repent (turn away from) of the things that have kept you from Him. Make your heart right with God today. It will be amazing how soon your season can change once your heart is right with God! You might still have the consequences of those sins or poor choices, but you will have God's presence and grace on your life as you walk through them.

**Have I made bad choices or been disobedient to God, and as a result, find myself in this season of famine?**

Through making wrong choices (like Elimelech), we can find ourselves in a famine season, and it's very hard to hear God's voice or feel His presence during these times. Making the choice to not forgive someone, or harboring anger, bitterness, or resentment in your heart will most certainly allow your spirit to run dry and your heart to harden. As a result, you will find yourself in a season of barrenness and dryness in your own soul. Release those things in your heart that are keeping you in the desert! There is not a person or situation worth you remaining in this famine season!

**Has God led me into this season of famine?**

There are times in our lives when we find ourselves in the desert simply because God has led us there. Jesus was led into the desert. Moses and the children of Israel were led through the desert even though they stayed longer than they needed to. Sometimes God wants us to walk in the desert for a while. He has a purpose for us being there. He wants to teach us, to grow in us, to work out some weakness in our life, or to make us more like Him.

Desert seasons are lonely times. As I look back over the desert seasons of my own life, I wouldn't trade them for anything. Those were the seasons when it felt like it was just me and God. When you're in the desert, you find yourself completely dependent on the One who led you there!

If you're in one of those seasons, I pray you find great comfort in the fact that the same Hand that led you TO the desert will be the same Hand that will lead you OUT of the desert! Trust that God is doing a work in you. Be attentive to His voice, be open to what He's pointing out in your heart, and be faithful to learn whatever lesson He longs to teach you. Our greatest times of growth and maturity don't happen on the mountain top seasons of our lives but in the dark, quiet, dry valley seasons that many times God is leading us through.

Elimelech's season of famine was clear though. He chose to leave the place of God in search of a new life for himself and his family. In times of hardship, he chose to walk away from God and into a coun-

try that didn't serve or acknowledge the God that Elimelech had once worshipped and loved.

The last sentence of Ruth 1:2 says, *"And they went to Moab and lived there."* Some versions say "they remained there". This family took up residence in a God-forsaken, outcast, wash pot country. They left the land God had placed them in because a difficult season came and brought a famine to their people. They packed up and left the "house of bread and praise".

While we cannot know the decision-making process in Elimelech's mind, what we do know is this: severe hardships and suffering followed their move to Moab. They lost everything. Naomi eventually lost her husband and two sons. Their family was lost and Naomi and her daughters-in-law were destitute without any hope or promise of a foreseeable future. She was left in a foreign land with two foreign girls dependent on her, and just when Naomi must have thought the days couldn't get any darker, they do. But God didn't leave Naomi. Though we don't read it on the pages of her story at this time, we feel it in the deepest places of our hearts. At the end of Naomi's story, we know that God's promises were true. HE. WAS. THERE! The God of Israel and of Naomi walked with her very personally and very closely. God truly *"worked all things together for her good"* (Romans 8:28). He allowed Naomi to leave the desert place where her husband had led her, and as we shall soon see, He lead her straight back into His purposes and plans for her life through a young girl who refused to leave her side…a girl named Ruth.

*discussion questions*

1. Up until this point in your life, what was your least favorite place to live? Explain why.

2. When you find yourself facing a difficult, dry season, what is your first instinct? Why?

3. Describe one of your famine seasons. What brought about that season?

4. Did you make mistakes or make wrong decisions during that season? Explain.

5. Go back to reread the three questions I asked you to consider during a famine season. Answer those questions honestly with your group or in your journal.

6. In looking back over famine seasons in your life, what are some of the invaluable lessons that you can now see God was teaching you as you navigated through that season?

7. If you are currently in a famine season, write out a prayer of confession and dependence upon your God Who is walking with you through this season. If you're on the other side of a famine season, write out a prayer of thankfulness and gratitude for the faithfulness of God leading you out of that season and the lessons that He taught you.

*chapter three*

# The Road Back Home

Ruth 1:3-7

*"Now Elimelech, Naomi's husband, died, and she was left with her two sons. They married Moabite women, one named Orpah and the other Ruth. After they had lived there about ten years, both Mahlon and Kilion also died, and Naomi was left without her two sons and her husband. Naomi and Ruth Return to Bethlehem. When Naomi heard in Moab that the Lord had come to the aid of his people by providing food for them, she and her daughters-in-law prepared to return home from there. With her two daughters-in-law she left the place where she had been living and set out on the road that would take them back to the land of Judah."*

There is nothing quite like pulling into the driveway of your HOME. Whether it be your own home, your parents home, or grandparents home, all the stress and anxiety of what that day may have held seems to slip off your shoulders and out of your mind as you turn your steering wheel towards HOME.

My husband has told me for years that no matter how awful or stressful his day gets, his thoughts in his mind are, "If I can just get home, everything will be ok." Isn't that so true? HOME...the sight, the smell, the feel, the memories resonate inside each one of us. Oh sure, there may be some not so great feelings and memories of home, but the good ones usually override the bad ones when we think of HOME.

Naomi had left her home a long time ago at this point. Ten years to be exact, and a lot had happened since leaving Bethlehem. After living in Moab for some time, Naomi's husband, Elimelech, died. Naomi was left with her two sons and their wives. The Bible goes on to tell us that ten years later, Naomi's two sons die. Her son's names were Mahlon, meaning "unhealthy" and Kilion, meaning "puny". Remember, Bible names had meanings of significance. It is probable that these two sons were born with some serious health issues, thus the names that were given to them. Naomi's name means "pleasant", and as we will read in later chapters, Naomi must have had a wonderful testimony in her homeland of Bethlehem because she was so pleasant and joyful even with the burden of unhealthy children.

Ten years is a long time to be in a desert season in a foreign land, but that's exactly where Naomi found herself. Remember how God's blessings will eventually follow our obedience? Now Naomi finds herself in a foreign land, with no husband, no sons, and two daughters-in-law totally dependent upon her. No pressure, right? It certainly doesn't look like God's blessings, does it?

In Bible times, there was nothing worse than becoming a widow. Widows were taken advantage of or ignored and were almost always poverty stricken. Women were not allowed to be educated, and they held the social status of little more than animals. God's law provided that the nearest relative to the dead husband take care of the widow, but Naomi had no relatives in Moab and didn't know if any of her own relatives were alive in Israel.

Can you imagine the state of hopelessness Naomi must have been in? Not only is she mourning the death of her husband and two sons, but she is also bearing the weight of responsibility for her two daughters-in-law in a foreign land that she probably didn't even want to be in!

Have you ever felt that desperate and hopeless? It is not just one tragedy happening; it is tragedy all around you. There are days when you can't even think straight for yourself, much less for the people around you. That's exactly where Naomi found herself. She was very desperate, and her days were very dark.

In the midst of all this, Naomi got some good news! Word got back to her that God had come to the rescue of her people in Bethlehem by providing food for them. (v.6) The famine was now over! So with that great news, the two girls and Naomi made plans to return to Naomi's homeland. Ten years later. A decade of sorrow and heartbreak. A decade of loneliness and isolation. A decade of possible resentment and grief towards a husband who had led his family to a God-forsaken country. Ten years is a long time to be in a famine season. But now, the season was about to change, and it was time for Naomi to go HOME.

I believe that verse 7 is one of the most hopeful verses in all of the book of Ruth. If verse 7 would not have happened, the rest of the story and God's promises would not have come to be. It tells us "with her two daughters-in-law she LEFT THE PLACE where she had been living and SET OUT ON THE ROAD that would take them back to the land of Judah."

**Seasons of famine can often get us off of the right road, but by the grace of God there is ALWAYS A ROAD BACK HOME!**

No matter how far you've strayed, how disobedient you've been, how many mistakes you've made, or how many consequences you've had to suffer, whether through your own fault or someone else's, God has prepared a road back home for you! It's your choice, however, to get in the driver's seat of your own life and drive yourself HOME.

Naomi, even in her season of despair and loss, in hopelessness and pain, had the wherewithal within her to know WHEN IT WAS TIME TO MOVE ON! IT. WAS. TIME. The season of mourning had subsided. The season of dryness had run its course. The season of separation from her people and homeland had come to its end. The season of loss and desperation had stopped. It was time to move on! Thank God Naomi had the determination and strength to GET UP AND

MOVE ON! It was that very step of moving on that eventually led to promise and provision, to purpose and destiny, and for all of history to be written - all because a woman, who found herself in the darkest days of her life, packed up and left the place she was and put herself back on the road that led her home!

I've seen far too many women over the years who have never learned the lesson that Naomi learned. Women who have "remained" in their Moab and refused to move on from a terrible tragedy or season of their lives. Please hear my heart on this: there are absolutely times of sorrow, mourning, and pain. It takes much prayer and time for those places in our hearts to heal, trusting that God is with us during our darkest days: losing a loved one, walking through betrayal of a friend or spouse, watching our own children lose their way, signing papers to finalize a divorce you never thought would happen, watching a career or dream die before your very eyes. We have all walked through great tragedy and loss. God is the Great Healer of our broken hearts, but our healing is something we cannot rush. It just takes time. As time passes and God faithfully begins to heal your heart, there comes a moment when each of us has to GET UP and MOVE ON. If not, we will remain and live in a season we were never intended to reside in, and as a result, we will stop living our lives. We will stop growing. We will stop dreaming. We will stop hoping and looking to the future because our future will have stopped at our last tragedy. We can't *"smile at the future"* or *"laugh at the days to come"* (Proverbs 31:25) because our lives will have stopped. Stopped at the last heartache or heartbreak. Stopped at the last disappointment. Just stopped. With no hope for our future.

What if Naomi had stopped? Not gotten up and moved on? I promise you we wouldn't be reading or studying her story. Without Naomi moving on, Ruth wouldn't have moved on. Without Ruth moving on, Boaz couldn't have redeemed her, and the lineage of Jesus quite possibly would have gone through another family line. But it didn't. All because Naomi got up and moved on and placed herself back on the road that led her home.

What story is waiting to be written in your life? What God-story is waiting for you to get up and move on?

You will never know that story and all the people it will affect and the history that can be made until you GET UP and MOVE ON.

Get back into the driver's seat of your life. Buckle your seat belt and turn your steering wheel towards HOME.

Just do it! You will be so glad you did because IT'S TIME TO MOVE ON!

# CHAPTER 3

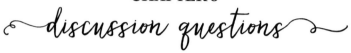

*discussion questions*

**1.** Share some of your fondest childhood memories of your home, or the home of a grandparent or family member. Why are those memories so special to you?

**2.** Can you relate to Naomi in her long season of famine and hopelessness? Why or why not?

**3.** Describe a time in your life when you had to make the decision to "get up and move on". Share some of the emotions and thought processes you had or felt in that decision.

**4.** Do you find yourself facing some of those same decisions today? What is it that you need to "move on" from?

**5.** Why do you think it's so hard for you to "move on"?

**6.** Take a moment now to confess to God (and to your small group) the place you need to leave to return back home. Make a declaration to turn your eyes to the place God has waiting for you, either literally or figuratively. Then start taking steps to get you to that place.

# Writing the Pages of History

*Ruth 1:8-14*

*"Then Naomi said to her two daughters-in-law, "Go back, each of you, to your mother's home. May the Lord show you kindness, as you have shown kindness to your dead husbands and to me. May the Lord grant that each of you will find rest in the home of another husband." Then she kissed them goodbye and they wept aloud and said to her, "We will go back with you to your people." But Naomi said, "Return home, my daughters. Why would you come with me? Am I going to have any more sons, who could become your husbands? Return home, my daughters; I am too old to have another husband. Even if I thought there was still hope for me - even if I had a husband tonight and then gave birth to sons - would you wait until they grew up? Would you remain unmarried for them? No, my daughters. It is more bitter for me than for you, because the Lord's hand has turned against me!" At this they wept aloud again. Then Orpah kissed her mother-in-law goodbye, but Ruth clung to her. "*

*W*omen do things in packs. Have you ever noticed that? We go to the restroom together, shop together, have coffee together, cry together, pray together, share child birth stories together (Why in the world do we do that? ☺). Women love being with other women. We just "get" each other. Men on the other hand? They don't necessarily "get" us. But other women? ABSOLUTELY, yes we do!

Even if Naomi wanted to go back to Bethlehem alone, she didn't have a choice! She had two daughters-in-law that obviously loved her very much, and she wasn't going anywhere without them. It didn't matter that these girls didn't know Naomi's country, lifestyle, culture, religion or ways. They were going, and there was no talking them out of it! Or so it seemed.

Until Orpah started thinking. Thinking about what she was about to do and what her future was going to look like. She then made a decision to stay in her own homeland of Moab, a land that was familiar, safe, and without risks. Yes, Orpah would stay put. But Ruth? She couldn't be talked out of it even if her life depended on it. She was willing to take the risk, to walk into the unknown, to be a foreigner in a strange land. Boy, did her decision pay off! But, let us back up just a little bit in the story.

In Ruth 1:8-14, we find the three women (remember we travel in packs ☺) standing at a crossroads in Moab. They were three women making decisions that would affect all of eternity. Obviously, they didn't know the impact of their decisions then, but we certainly know the impact of their decisions now. Three women, hugging and crying together. Three women who have been through a lot of tragedy together and shared heartache and loss. All three have lost their husbands. By losing their husbands, they lost their hope for a bright, financially secure future. Isn't it amazing how a tragedy can bring hearts together? Or possibly tear hearts apart? We have the choice of how we allow a tragedy to affect us, and these three women chose to cling closely to each other because no one else knew exactly how they felt or what heart wrenching decisions lay before them.

Naomi tries to dissuade these two girls from going back to Bethlehem with her. She explains to them what the situation will be like if they go with her. The Israelites and Moabites had nothing to do with one another. Remember, Moab was a fierce enemy of Israel. Naomi tells them that because they are Moabites, it would cost them everything to go to Bethlehem with her. It was bad enough that they were widows. By going with Naomi, they would be widows in a foreign land, from a country that Israel had great hostility towards.

At first, even after Naomi's desperate plea for them to stay, both girls insisted on going with her. However, after more persuasion, Orpah decided to remain in her homeland of Moab. Orpah chose to go back to her home and her family, but Ruth could not be persuaded. At the time, it may not have looked like an important decision, but the decision made that day affected all of eternity!

In verse 14 it says, *"Then Orpah kissed her mother-in-law good bye..."* and that is the last we hear of her.

**Orpah walked off the pages of the Bible,
never to be heard from again.**

Orpah had relatives in Moab, family that could provide for her. The God of Israel was not the god of Moab. The Moabites worshipped false gods, and Orpah stayed with her gods, her familiar, risk-free life, her culture, and customs.

I think Orpah gets a bad rap for her decision that day, but, honestly, would any of us have done differently? Sure, we are full of faith and courage reading their story now, and it is easy to say, "No way! I would have gone with Naomi!" But if you were in Orpah's shoes, would you really have chosen differently?

Most of the decisions in our lives boil down to safety or surrender. What's easiest for me? What's the safe, familiar, and comfortable decision to make? What's the route with the least risks to take? Often times, we take that road, the safe, dependable, no-risk road. We become just like Orpah. Not making history, not writing our God-story, not thinking of how our decisions will influence others, only thinking of how our decision will affect us. We are really not all that different from Orpah. Orpah chose to stay in Moab, and we choose to stay in our nice, comfortable, predictable lives. We walk off the pages of history, never to be heard from again either.

There is very little difference at all between Orpah and us.

Our Christian lives are not supposed to be about safety. They are supposed to be about surrender. They shouldn't be about self-preservation but about self-sacrifice. Sounds a little bit like Jesus, doesn't it? In the New Testament, Jesus tells us to lay our own lives down and to pick up His cross and that our lives are not lived for ourselves but for Him. (Matthew 16:34)

Many, many years ago, I had graduated high school and was soon to leave for bible college. I knew bible college was where I was to go because at age fourteen, I felt God asking me to give my life to full-time ministry. I answered a scary but wholehearted "yes" to Him. Because I grew up in a very small town and in a close-knit family, leaving home was no easy decision. I was the first person in my family to go to college. The day I left for college, I knew in my heart I would never be back. Back for visits, yes. Back to live, no. I knew God was asking something more of me. I was at a crossroads and I had to make a decision. He was asking for a totally surrendered life - a life, looking back now, that I could have only dreamed of. However, it wasn't a life without pain and heartache. It was a life of self-sacrifice and surrender; it was a life that not everyone was going to understand.

Ministry was a great unknown to that eighteen year old girl. At the time, very few people in my family were Christians, much less in ministry. I wasn't following in any family members' footsteps; I was walking a road where there were no footprints at all. I had made a decision to follow God and His calling on my life. I decided to surrender my will to His will not realizing at the time how deeply that decision would affect me, and eventually, my future husband and children. My family couldn't understand that decision and the sacrifice it would take, even to this day. That decision meant I would never live in my hometown again. It meant I couldn't make visits home as often as my family would have liked. It also meant that people's perception of me would be that I had chosen God and ministry over my extended family. Nothing was further from the truth. Self-sacrifice isn't something that everyone understands or embraces.

I can relate to Orpah and the decision set before her, but I can also relate to Ruth. Her purpose and destiny depended on the decision she made that day to cling tightly to Naomi.

Sacrifice isn't a word we like to use for ourselves. We don't like to sacrifice anything. We want it all: God's love, grace, blessings, and forgiveness, but we don't want to give up anything. We want to live our own lives, our own way while still asking God to bless and prosper us. We want to write our own stories with our own plots and our own happy endings. Very seldom do our stories turn out the way we would have written them.

Many of the crossroads in our own lives are found at the exact place where Orpah faced her crossroads decision. Will we lay our lives down and surrender to the life God has asked of us? Or will we remain in the familiar, secure, and predictable life that we have written out for ourselves?

It is your own decision. No one will make it for you, not even God.

**History is only made and God-stories
are only written with lives that are completely and totally
surrendered to Him.**

Will you continue writing the pages of history? Or will you, like Orpah, walk off history's pages, never to be heard from again?

God has left that decision up to you…and to me.

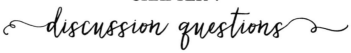
*discussion questions*

**1.**  Share some of the God relationships that He has placed in your life. Why are those relationships so important to you?

**2.**  Describe a time in your life when you faced a crossroad and had to make a difficult decision. What things did you consider in making that decision?

**3.**  Looking back, did you make the right decision? Why or why not?

**4.**  Share an experience when you were faced with choosing personal safety verses personal surrender or self-preservation verses sacrifice?

**5.**  Which did you choose and why? Was it the correct decision and why?

**6.**  What changes do you need to make in your life to begin living a life of total surrender to God? Are you willing to make those changes? If not, why not?

**7.**  Speak to someone in your small group or a trusted friend about the changes you desire to make in your life in order to live a surrendered life to God and His plans for you. Ask them to hold you accountable as you walk out these steps of change.

# Find your People, Find your Purpose

*Ruth 1:14*
*"At this they wept aloud again. Then Orpah kissed her*
*mother-in-law goodbye, but Ruth clung to her."*

**R**uth was a determined young woman. She could not be persuaded to leave Naomi, no matter how difficult a life she was walking into. I can appreciate that. I am a bit of a determined woman myself. In fact, my husband has told me over the years, "Heidi, you are the most determined woman I've ever met!" I don't know whether he meant it as a compliment or not?☺ Determined can also mean stubborn. However, to be determined is a good thing, to be stubborn is not.

Ruth was most certainly determined. Even the Bible states in verse 18, "When Naomi realized that Ruth was determined to go with her, she stopped urging her." There was no talking Ruth out of going with

Naomi. It was not going to happen. As Orpah kissed Naomi and said her good-byes (verse 14), Ruth clung to Naomi. There was something about her relationship with Naomi that Ruth was not going to let go of. What Ruth didn't realize at that moment was that Naomi didn't just represent a new life and new culture for Ruth. Naomi represented the divine purpose and destiny Ruth was about to walk into.

**RUTH'S PURPOSE AND DESTINY WAS A PERSON at that moment, and she clung to her.**

Ruth wasn't letting go.

The same is true for us as well. Ecclesiastes 4:9 tells us that *"Two are better than one"*. God never intended for us to walk through life or discover His purpose alone. Our God-given purpose and destiny are found within the very people that God has called us to walk with.

We often say this phrase at our church, "When you find your people, you find your purpose," and it is so very true. We ask God to reveal His purpose to us, but our purpose is found in the people we are connected to. So our prayer should really be, "God, show me the people you want me to walk with, to connect with, to build your kingdom with," and through our divine God connecting relationships with the right people, God reveals His purpose to us!

Look at Ruth. Her purpose was found in the person she was divinely connected to. She didn't know it at the time. She just knew the person she was to walk with and stay connected to was her mother-in-law

Naomi. Because of Ruth's relationship and connection with Naomi, Ruth was led right into her God-given purpose!

I grew up in a small country town in Texas. The population was 6,000 people in its prime. My family attended a small country church. It was a wonderful church with wonderful people. It was the pastor, his wife, and their children that really grabbed my heart. I loved them. They treated and loved me as one of their own family members, and I loved them equally the same way. The pastors' children and I were all around the same age, so we grew up together in school and in church. Because the pastors' family loved God's house and His people, this is where MY love for God's house and His people began. Some of my fondest memories are of my years at our church with my pastor, his wife, and children. Looking back, I now know that my pastors saw something in me that I did not see in myself. They saw a young teenage girl with a lot of rough edges, but they also saw a girl that had a God-calling on her life. They allowed me to teach children's church, to speak to my youth group, to help in any and every way that I could. And trust me, I volunteered for everything! I just loved our church, and I loved my pastors with all my heart!

My pastors' two older children were a few years older than me, so when it came time for them to go to college, I was so sad. But I was determined (there's that word again!) in my heart that wherever my pastors' children (also some of my dearest friends, even to this day) went to college, I would go too. It didn't matter which college it was or where it was, I was going where they went! Two years later, I did exactly that. They could not get rid of me even if they had tried!

It was at this bible college years later that I met and eventually married my husband. If I had not clung to my pastors and their children, I would not have ended up where I needed to be and would not have met my future husband. When you find your people, you really do find your purpose! That principle has played out over and over again during my life. I've had pastors, leaders, and divine relationships that God placed in my life. He used them to lead me directly into my own life's purpose and destiny. It would not have happened without PEOPLE!

You cannot say you love God, but you don't love His people. The entire Bible is a story about relationships: God's relationship to us, our relationship to Him, His relationship to the world, and our relationships with one another. We just cannot escape it! We were created to walk with one another. Often times, we are looking and asking God for the wrong thing. We are longing for purpose and destiny to be revealed to us, but God desires to connect us through relationships with His people. There we will find His purposes for our lives!

I don't think Ruth had any idea what she was doing when she clung to Naomi. She was just her mother-in-law whom she loved deeply. But as Ruth and Naomi left Moab and journeyed to Bethlehem, unknowingly, they were both walking into the greatest purpose and destiny of their entire lives! God was about to turn years and years of famine and heartache into a lifetime of provision, blessings, and a secure future. History was about to be written through the lives of two women whom God had joined together.

# CHAPTER 5

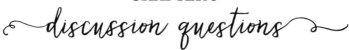

*discussion questions*

1. In your opinion, explain the difference between determined and stubborn. Which one are you?

2. Explain to your small group (or write in your journal) how the God relationships in your life have influenced you in walking into His purposes and plans for you.

3. Have you been faithful to nurture those relationships in your life? Why or why not? How can you improve?

4. Take some time this week to make a phone call, send a note, or set up a lunch with those divine relationships to let them know your appreciation of their role in your life.

# Let Your Answer Be Yes

*Ruth 1:16-18*

*But Ruth replied, "Don't urge me to leave you or to turn back from you. Where you go I will go, and where you stay I will stay. Your people will be my people and your God my God. Where you die I will die, and there I will be buried. May the Lord deal with me, be it ever so severely, if even death separates you and me." When Naomi realized that Ruth was determined to go with her, she stopped urging her.*

*O*ur sweet, determined Ruth had some big decisions to make even before moving to Bethlehem with Naomi. It wasn't just one decision, but several decisions she had to say "yes" to before leaving her homeland. Remember, Ruth was now going to be the foreigner. She had never been to Bethlehem, Judah. She had only heard of this new land and could have never imagined what was waiting for her on the other side. It must have been scary for her to leave her family, her lifestyle, her homeland, her friends, her religion, and her gods. But again, determination is what gave her the strength to say, "Naomi, I'm going with you, and I cannot be talked out of it!"

Ruth made several decisions and verbal declarations of her intent when responding to Naomi's attempt to persuade her to stay in Moab.

## 1) "Where you will go, I will go"

Ruth made a decision to go with Naomi, no matter what the uncertainty of her future looked like. She could not be dissuaded. Just like I said to my pastors' children, "whatever college y'all go to…guess what? I'm going too!"

## 2) "Where you lodge, I will lodge"

Ruth wasn't going to just get Naomi safely to Bethlehem, drop her off, and then return back to Moab. Ruth was staying. This was not a vacation for Ruth. She was making a life-long commitment to Naomi. Through this statement, Ruth was renouncing her homeland; she was turning away from her old way of life. She was going to be identified with Naomi and would accept all that Naomi was going to face as a widow upon her return to Bethlehem.

Ruth's decision was not temporary. It was for a lifetime.

### 3) "Your people will be my people"

Ruth's decision was to leave her own people and to become identified with God's people. Not only was Ruth embracing a new land, she was also embracing the people of this new land. To love God is to love the people of God. Jesus tells us so in the Great Commandment (Matthew 22:37-39). Ruth chose to embrace the people of God before she ever met them. She made a decision to allow Naomi's "people" to become her "people" as well.

### 4) "Your God will be my God"

Wow! This one is pretty powerful! Ruth was choosing to follow a God she did not even know yet but had obviously seen Him through the life of Naomi. Because of what she had seen in Naomi, Ruth made a decision to follow that God.

Can the same be said of us? Will people in our lives be so moved and touched by the God they only know of because of our lives? Would they want to serve Him as well? Naomi's God was not one Ruth had experienced for herself. She had only heard of Him. Yet, she vowed to serve and follow Him all because of a woman in her life named Naomi, that represented Him so well.

### 5) "Where you will die, I will die"

Ruth made a promise to Naomi for the rest of her life. This was not just for convenience until things got better for her. This was for FOR-EVER! Our true character is revealed when we face a crisis moment. Ruth was at a crisis moment in her life, and her character and heart shone brightly.

Orpah loved Naomi also, and for a while there seemed to be no difference between the two girls. However, when the moment of decision arrived, the difference became very clear.

### 6 "and there I will be buried"

Ruth's promise to Naomi didn't allow for any association with her old relationships or lifestyle prior to her knowing the one, true God. Again, there was no turning back for Ruth. It is no wonder that God honored Ruth the way He did. Through her decisions, He saw Ruth's heart of commitment towards Naomi and her God.

### 7 "May the Lord deal with me...if anything but death separates us"

This was a decision Ruth made that brought her to the end of her own will and plans for her life.

What Ruth didn't know then, was that her commitment to Naomi was really a commitment to her God. God honored Ruth, through Ruth's honoring of Naomi.

What's astounding to me about Ruth's decisions is that she made these choices and declarations BEFORE she ever arrived in Bethlehem! She didn't wait until she got there to make them. She didn't wait to see if she felt like it, nor did she wait to see what life was going to be like before making these choices. She made her life-changing choices before seeing what the outcome was going to be.

Don't wait on a feeling or clear picture of the future before you answer "yes". Ruth stated over and over again "I WILL…" , not "Let me see how I feel," or "Let's see how this new life plays out for me, then I'll decide". She declared her commitment to Naomi, which ultimately was a commitment to God, before she ever knew what her new life and future would look like. We would do well to learn from Ruth because that is some serious FAITH.

Are you willing to answer "yes" to whatever God may be asking of you? Are you willing to answer "yes" before you even know what His question or request of you will be?

I WILL.

God never asks anything of us that He hasn't already done Himself.

God has made some declarations over you as well.

In Psalm 91:14-16, God beautifully says to us:

> *"Because he loves me," says the Lord, 'I will rescue him;*
> *I will protect him, for he acknowledges my name.*

*He will call upon me, and I will answer him;*
*I will be with him in trouble,*
*I will deliver him and honor him.*
*With long life will I satisfy him*
*And show him my salvation."*

His word promises us that He will rescue, protect, answer, walk with, deliver, satisfy, and reveal His salvation to us. What a promise He has made to us!

Take comfort in the words of your Heavenly Father as He speaks His commitments and promises over you.

# CHAPTER 6

## discussion questions

1. Describe your biggest geographical move thus far in your life. What were some obstacles you faced in making the decision of that move? What were some of the benefits?

2. Are you glad that you made that move? Explain why. If not, why?

3. Have you ever visited another country? If so, how did you adjust to the culture? Did you feel like an outsider? How so?

4. Why do you think adjusting to new cultures or customs is so difficult?

5. Place yourself in Ruth's shoes for a moment. What would have been your thought process in choosing to go with Naomi to a new country with its new cultures and customs?

6. Are you facing some "I will" decisions in your life now? Share the details of that decision with your small group.

7. Read aloud Psalm 91:14-16 (with your small group, or alone). Take comfort in all that God promises to you and conclude with a prayer of thanksgiving for those promises.

# chapter seven

# Mothers and Daughters

*Psalm 34:18*
*"The Lord is close to the brokenhearted and saves those*
*who are crushed in spirit."*

**H**ave you ever broken something that was very special to you? A family heirloom? A favorite antique vase? A treasured piece of china? It seems as if the more delicate the object, the more pieces it breaks into.

I once dropped a favorite dish, and broken pieces of glass and shard flew everywhere! Your heart is shattered as you see your most treasured possession scattered in a million pieces without any hope of putting it back together. Whether it's a broken vase or a broken heart, the pieces of shard have the ability to hurt those closest to the broken object or person.

Broken things create sharp pieces of shard. A shard is the sharp piece of glass that is broken off of an object. Shards can create damage and pain, and they cut deep. Very deep. Not only in inanimate objects, but also in people. I know that first hand. I have seen the damage of brokenness in a family and in a mother-daughter relationship because I am not only a mother, I am also a daughter.

**Mother-daughter relationships can be heaven on earth...or not.**

It depends on the level of untended brokenness in both hearts or the level of invited healing in the heart of both the mother and of the daughter.

Brokenness does not mean hopelessness. It means that something or someone is "damaged, or not working properly". Broken people either intentionally or unintentionally hurt other people. Like shattered shard, they can be sharp and painful to everyone in their path, especially those closest to them.

Broken mothers have the ability to create broken daughters. Whole mothers also have the ability to create whole daughters. Being whole does not mean perfect, it simply means 'not broken'. Broken people do not just become whole. They must first see their brokenness and the pain they are bringing to others. Broken people do not become healed by ignoring their own brokenness. They are healed by honestly recognizing their brokenness and bringing the broken pieces of their hearts to a God who can put them back together.

Brokenness cuts deep into our own hearts and into the hearts of the ones we love. I think all of us carry a level of brokenness in our lives that we need God to heal, but the cycle can be and must be stopped. It can be stopped by mothers and by daughters through much forgiveness and by even more grace.

Wholeness can come to your heart, so much so, that your brokenness isn't even recognizable anymore.

**Daughters replicate what they see in their mothers, the brokenness or the wholeness. As mothers, we have the choice as to which one it will be.**

Naomi felt the pain of brokenness, so did Ruth, and so did I.

Both Naomi and Ruth pushed past their deepest places of brokenness and allowed God to heal those areas so that they could eventually walk as healthy, whole women. By the grace of God, so have I.

All families experience a certain level of brokenness, but it is what they do with it that determines whether they remain broken or whether they journey to a place of wholeness. The book of Ruth certainly does not give us the details of how Naomi and Ruth received their healing, but we see a clear shift, especially in Naomi, from whom she was in Chapter 1 to the woman she became in Chapters 2-4.

Naomi must have been a really great mother-in-law for Ruth to love her so deeply and refuse to be separated from her. I have a really great mother-in- law too. For over twenty-seven years, my mother-in-law has loved and treated me like her own daughter. I am so blessed, and so was Ruth.

The Bible tells us nothing of Ruth's biological family. We know nothing of her parents, siblings, grandparents, or cousins, but we do know they were all Moabites: a people hostile to the nation of Israel, to its people, and to their God. We don't know if Ruth took grief from her family for marrying a Jewish man. Given the history between these two countries, I think we can safely draw the conclusion that Ruth's family may not have been too happy about this marital union. Maybe that is why Ruth clung so tightly to Naomi. Perhaps Ruth's family disowned her for her choice of a spouse from Israel. Maybe that is why Ruth had no desire to remain in Moab with her family, even after desperate pleas from Naomi for her to stay. Orpah had no problem going back and staying with her family, her country, and her people. Ruth, on the other hand, acted as if staying in Moab was never even an option for her. Was it because she had no family to go back to? Had they washed their hands of her because of her union and association with the Israelites and their God?

We can only assume these things about Ruth. I can certainly relate, though. I can relate because of my decision to answer "yes" to the God-calling on my life and a life of ministry. Most times my parents, in particular my mother, just could not understand.

Like I said earlier, when I left home at eighteen, I knew I was never going back. Don't get me wrong, I loved my family and friends; I loved my hometown; I loved my church and church family. I have very fond memories of growing up in our small, Texas town, and there are still days that I miss it. I miss what used to be, but I think even more so, I miss what could have been.

My parents were both raised in homes with great struggles and hardships. I don't know all the details of their upbringing because we didn't talk about things like that, but I do know it was hard for them. They were both the oldest children of large families and both carried a lot of financial weight and responsibility of working at young ages to help make ends meet at home. When my parents met, and eventually married, they decided they wanted to raise their family in a way that they had never been raised themselves. For that, I am very grateful.

Growing up, it seemed as if there was not a time that my mother was at peace with everyone in her life. I now know it was because her heart was broken, very broken.

My father, on the other hand, was the peacekeeper of the family, not the peacemaker. There is a difference - a big difference. A peacemaker is one who will deal with whatever or whoever needs to be addressed to make sure that peace is present and not robbed within the home. A peacekeeper is one who will not deal with what needs to be dealt with because of fear of rocking the boat and crossing the person who is continually robbing the peace or creating the non-peaceful atmosphere.

My family walked on eggshells a lot. All of us. I thought this was normal. As a child growing up, I too would find myself as a peacekeeper. I hated people being mad at each other. I hated family members not speaking to one another, and that was a constant in my family. I would always try to "fix" the situation. I would talk to all people involved, trying to get things resolved, desperately wanting peace within our own family and extended family. I remember the knots that I would feel in my stomach when family members weren't right with each other, and the majority of the time my mother was always involved in some way or another.

Looking back, I assume I did this because I was the oldest child. The oldest child sometimes assumes responsibility that we should never assume. I continued to carry that responsibility of "keeping the peace" within my family, and many, many years later, that weight of responsibility almost crushed me. It became more than any human being should be expected to carry. God never put that responsibility on me, nor did my family. I put it on myself. Sadly, I did not figure that out until years later.

Once I married and eventually had a family of my own, I began to realize that this was not normal behavior at all. In fact, it was dysfunctional. Very unhealthy, very broken, and very painful. I once heard someone describe dysfunction as "when something is broken but no one knows how to fix it." That pretty much describes my family. All families are broken in some way. All families disappoint and fail one another. All families face times of hardship and pain, but functional families take responsibility in what is broken within their family unit and either fix it themselves or seek outside help to fix it. By fixing it, I don't mean to make it perfect. I mean to recognize and address the problems, give and receive much forgiveness and grace, continue to love one another through the season of "fixing" the brokenness, and get up and move on in a healthy way allowing God's grace to cover and heal everyone involved.

Dysfunctional families do not see the brokenness, or they do see it and choose not to address it or even acknowledge that it's there. They ignore it, blame others for it, or keep silent about it. As time goes by, more things within the family break, and more dysfunction happens. Then one day, it all breaks down, and the question arises, "Can this even be fixed at all now?" There is no family beyond repair, but all family members have to recognize the dysfunction and be willing to get help for their brokenness. If not, it stays broken for a long time, possibly even a lifetime.

As a young wife, (pastor's wife at that) and young mother, I began to see what was normal through my relationships with my in-laws, my church family and friends, and by the grace of God. It wasn't perfect, but normal. I also began to see what abnormal was and that abnormal defined my relationship with my mother.

I remember the phone calls from my mother that would come in my early years of marriage and parenting. It was usually about the drama within the family. I would hang the phone up with the weight of what felt like an elephant on my chest, trying to figure out how I could fix it or who I needed to call to help make things better within

my extended family. This went on for years and eventually began to affect the peace of God within my own home, marriage, and family. It was after one of those phone calls that my husband, who had basically come to the end of his patience with me and my mother, spoke the words that forever changed how I looked at my family situation. He said to me, "Heidi, you did not break them, so you certainly cannot fix them!" Those words were like a slap of reality right in my face! I now know they were really words from the heart of God to bring me freedom from the responsibility and crushing weight I had carried for my family my entire life.

Though I had not created the dysfunction and brokenness of my family, I did experience the consequences of it. Now granted, as a zealous, passionate teenager with an outgoing, loud personality I may have contributed to some of the craziness and drama, ☺ but I had certainly not caused the dysfunction in my family. The brokenness in the life of my mother had happened long before I came along. Looking back, I now know that she was never at peace with herself, which made it impossible for her to be at peace with others. Because I did not cause the brokenness in my extended family, I certainly didn't have the power to fix their brokenness. Only God could do that, and I was not God.

Those words from my husband were one of the God-moments in my life where I felt freedom and hope from the brokenness of my family, perhaps for the first time. It was also through that God-moment I realized that most of how I had navigated my relationship with my mother was out of guilt. I had operated from a place of guilt, not from a place of truth and faith.

Over the years, I have come to realize that God does not place guilt on us in order to change us, but he does use the conviction of the Holy Spirit. Guilt is used by the enemy to bring condemnation to our hearts and to have us act out of feeling bad instead of acting out of principle and conviction. **God does not motivate us out of guilt to get us to do something.** He gently, but firmly, brings conviction to our hearts to redirect or correct us. It is always out of love, never out of guilt. This is a lesson that took me many years to finally learn.

I know that my parents did the best they knew to do in raising my siblings and I. They gave us a life they never had themselves. I am very thankful to them for that. I fault them for nothing. I just cannot fix their brokenness. Because of the severe brokenness in the heart of my mother, she mothered out of that brokenness and pain, not even realizing what she was doing to her own daughters. The gift that it has been to me, (yes, a gift!) is that I have seen first hand how brokenness, unforgiveness, hurt, and pain can manifest into the lives of those you are closest to and the damage the sharp shards of brokenness can inflict. You can either face those pains and wounds in your heart and allow God to heal them, or you can ignore them and act as if they aren't there and allow yourself to hurt and eventually separate yourself from the people you love the most.

Sadly, my mother chose the latter. She chose separation from the ones closest to her and those whom I know she loved deeply.

I am not a victim, and I am not lacking in any way. God has made up any lack in my life and the lives of my children through the divine relationships He has brought into our lives. I made a decision a long time ago, that my daughters would not have to face the pain and heartache that I've had to face in the mother-daughter relationship. Had I not allowed God to touch and heal those tender places in my own heart, I would have parented out of my wounds and caused terrible pain in the relationship with my own daughters. I was determined (that word again!) not to allow that to happen. By the grace of God, it hasn't. I certainly haven't been a perfect mother, but I've been a "whole and healthy" mother. I have allowed God to heal the brokenness in my own heart. My healing hasn't come without much hurt and pain, but it has come. Slowly and surely. God's healing touch has come to my heart.

My daughters will never know the pain of not having a mother in their lives. That would not have happened had I not allowed God into the deepest, most painful places of my heart and allowed Him to remain there and work there.

Because I did, healing has come. I don't hate my mother. I love her, truly. I just hate what unresolved brokenness, pain, unforgiveness, and heartache can do to a family. God never intended it to be that way.

It was originally TD Jakes who once said, "Out of your greatest misery will come your greatest ministry." That is certainly the case in my life. My greatest place of pain has become my greatest place of purpose. I've spent my entire adult life becoming to other women what I have so deeply longed for in my own life: having a healthy relationship with my mother. I'm not only a physical mother to my own children, but I have purposed in my heart to be a spiritual mother to so many young girls and women who have so desperately needed one. That was never my plan for myself, but it was certainly God's plan for me and has been one of the greatest joys of my life.

A mother. A healthy, whole, and healed mother. It's amazing what God can do with the brokenness we bring to Him. He really can turn into good what the "enemy meant for evil". I am living proof of that!

**Mothers:** Please allow God to heal the broken areas in your hearts. God has created you as the influencer of your family and as Proverbs 4:23 tells us, *"Above all else, guard your heart, for it is the wellspring of life"*. Everything you allow to remain in your heart, the good and the bad, will eventually affect the people closest to you, in particularly, your family members.

I understand that it's painful to see the broken things within your own heart, but I also have seen firsthand what happens to a family when those areas are not dealt with. God is with you. He wants to not only lovingly point those areas out to you, but He also longs to come and touch your heart and heal your pain. It's not an overnight fix, but if you'll stay faithful to allow Him to work in those places of your heart, God will bring a healing to your heart like you've never thought possible. Trust me. I know. He's done it for me.

**Daughters:** Please give your mothers some grace! They simply did the best they knew to do in raising you. Raising daughters is a hard job. Most likely, your mother may have some wounds and pains in her own heart from her upbringing. Those were different days and times back then. People did not talk a lot about the "issues" of their hearts like we do today. Grace her in the fact that she loves you very much and is so proud of you, whether you hear those words from her mouth or not. Just trust that she feels those things in her heart.

If you've walked through a difficult relationship with your mother, release your pain, disappointment, unforgiveness, and resentment to God. He'll take it and heal it if you allow Him to. Your mother honestly did the best she could or wanted to do. You may not know the road she's walked or the pain she carries. It's not worth you having a hardened heart because you're not willing to forgive your mother. Just release her to God. You didn't break her, so you cannot fix her. Love and honor her. By doing so, it doesn't mean all that she has done is right. It just means you love and honor the position she has held in your life. You love and honor the right things she's done, and if you look closely, there are some right things there.

Finally, Daughters: use all that you've learned and walked through with your mother as a gift to know what to do and what not to do in raising your own daughters. Be purposeful and deliberate in being a great mother. You're not going to be perfect, but you can be great in the eyes of your children. Tell them you love them and how proud you are of them. Do not parent out of your own hurt and pain. Parent out of a healthy, whole heart for God. If you do, one day, your children will *"rise up and call you blessed"*. (Proverbs 31: 28)

If you have a healthy and whole mother, let her know how grateful you are for her! Do not take that relationship for granted. Let her know what she means to you and how grateful you are for a mother who loved you well!

If after reading this chapter, you have realized there is a mother wound in your heart, please pray this prayer with me. Even if your mother has passed away, if you now recognize the wound that has been left in your heart, you can also pray this prayer as a final release of forgiveness to her.

# dear Heavenly Father

I thank You for the mother You gave me. While she has not been perfect, I now realize she did the best she could given her circumstances and upbringing. I release forgiveness and grace to my mother. I will no longer hold unforgiveness towards her. I totally and completely release her to You, as I also release my hurt and my pain to You.

I refuse to allow the pain she has brought to me to control me any longer. You sent Your Son, Jesus, to take that pain with Him to the cross so that I would not have to carry it. I give that pain to You.

I will no longer allow my broken or fragmented relationship with my mother to affect my life and my future. I pray You work in her heart as You are working in mine. I ask that I will walk forward in hope, in grace, and in forgiveness. I will no longer look back but will look forward, into the great and hopeful future You have promised me.

I ask for healing to come to my heart and to the heart of my mother.

Thank you God for the hope and promise you have given me for my future and for my family. I make a choice to see my upbringing as a gift from You, and I commit to make the necessary changes in my family so that we can walk in health and wholeness, not dysfunction and brokenness.

Thank You for the release in my heart and for the healing that is to come.

amen

# CHAPTER 7

## discussion questions

1.  Describe your relationship with your mother. (Even if she has passed away, what did your relationship look like when she was alive?) Is that a relationship you would want to emulate with your own daughters? Why or why not?

2.  Are there areas of improvement with your relationship with your mother? How can you assist in those improvements?

3.  Describe your relationship with your mother-in-law (if you have one). What role has she played in your life? Are there areas of improvement with that relationship? How can you assist in those improvements?

4.  Would you describe yourself as a peacemaker or peacekeeper? Explain.

5.  Would you consider your upbringing as being part of a dysfunctional family or functional family? Explain why.

6.  Even as an adult, what are some of the current challenges you face within your extended family today? What are you doing to improve those challenges? Or not doing?

**7.** What was the greatest revelation you received out of this chapter?

**8.** Write a letter to your mother (living or passed away). Say anything you wish to say to her and everything you only hoped you could say. Give forgiveness. Give grace. Give thankfulness. Leave nothing left unsaid, but do so from a pure heart.

*Now prayerfully decide if you are to mail that letter to your mother. If it would be healing to her and to you, mail it full of faith, praying that healing would indeed come. If not, after writing the letter, bring it to God in prayer. Release it to God, along with the emotions you poured into it. Then throw it away, never to revisit it again, in total and complete release.*

*chapter eight*

# What is a Spiritual Daughter?

*Titus 2:3-5 (NLT)*

*"Similarly, teach the older women to live in a way that honors God. They must not slander others or be heavy drinkers. Instead, they should teach others what is good. These older women must train the younger women to love their husbands and their children, to live wisely and be pure, to work in their homes, to do good, and to be submissive to their husbands. Then they will not bring shame on the word of God."*

Ruth may have only been a daughter to Naomi by marriage, but she was really so much more than that. Ruth was a spiritual daughter in every sense of the word. She recognized the God-given relationship in Naomi, she honored that relationship, and she refused to be talked out of it.

**Ruth realized that she needed someone in her life
to help her walk down a road in a relationship with a God that she
had only heard of. Naomi was the person to do just that.**

As women, we all need "Ruths" in our lives, but we also need the "Naomis". It's important for us to connect with the younger women in our worlds, not only in age, but in spiritual journeys as well. Young women are looking for someone to take them by the hand and help them navigate the world in which we live. When we embrace the Ruth generations, it helps us to walk as Naomis before them. We also need the Naomi generations for their wisdom and godly instruction in our lives. If the only role we walk in is Ruth's, we can become needy, only taking from others, remaining on the receiving end of wisdom, counsel, and instruction. If we only walk in the role of a Naomi, we can become prideful, only giving our wisdom and counsel, but never placing ourselves in the position to receive from others. Both perspectives and positions are necessary.

Ruth is a beautiful example of a young girl that was open and embraced all that Naomi had to give her. We live in a time when people don't want to be told what to do. We know what's best for us. We want to do things our way. Ruth was the exact opposite. She was a strong, determined girl, but she was open for any direction and guidance Naomi had to give her. We would do well to learn from her example.

Throughout the book of Ruth, we see Ruth position herself as a "daughter" over and over. Here are some of her examples:

66

# What is a Spiritual Daughter?

**1)** **Ruth recognized whom God had divinely placed in her life, and she positioned herself closely to receive. (Ruth 1:6-10)**

Ruth took on the responsibility to stay close to Naomi. Not one time do we see Naomi seeking after Ruth or looking to see where she was. Ruth remained close.

Over my lifetime in ministry, I have not always had those "Naomis" up close and personal. For many years, I positioned myself as a Ruth from a distance. Twenty-seven years ago, women in ministry (or up-front, public ministry) were not as common as it is today. I did not have older, wiser women in my life that took an interest in me and helped me walk the road of full-time ministry. So I "stayed close" to women from a distance. Meaning I read all the books I could get my hands on. I listened to cassette tapes of women in leadership (I am dating myself now! ☺ ). I watched other women in ministry from a distance and gleaned what I could from their lives.

All these years later, I still purpose in my heart to walk as a Ruth. I should always be learning and gleaning from others. I don't know it all, and I continue to position my heart as a "daughter".

I have also walked as a Naomi. Nothing in the world blesses my heart more than young women, physically and spiritually, who continue to stay close to me and learn. I will walk a thousand miles with someone who will stay close and have an open heart for guidance, wisdom, and instruction. It is a joy for me! What becomes burdensome are those women who say they want a relationship, counsel, or wisdom, but are the same ones who I constantly have to chase after and remind them of their requests of me. They don't stay close. They say one thing with their mouths, but when it is time to put those words into action, they are nowhere to be found. That is not the heart of a Ruth. Ruth took responsibility for her own life and growth and stayed close...very close.

### 2) Ruth was not concerned for only herself, she submitted to another woman. (Ruth 1:11-13)

The word "submit" is not a popular word in our culture today...not at all! To submit doesn't mean to get run over and lose your influence. It simply means to "defer to another or prefer another's opinion". Whether it be your husband, your leaders or pastors, your friends, etc., the Bible also tells us to *"submit to one another"* (Ephesians 5:21) or to defer to others and their thoughts and opinions.

When you are in the middle of a situation, it is very hard for you to see it clearly, no matter how hard you try. You may have the best intentions but because you are too close, you just cannot see it clearly enough to make a good decision or judgment. When I am speaking a message on this topic, I use the illustration of my Bible. No matter how much I love the Bible, love to read the Bible, and have a heart to listen to what the Bible says about my particular situation, if I lay the Bible on my face, I cannot clearly see what it's telling me to do because I am just too close.

The same is true of you and whatever situation you may be facing. You can be so close to it that you cannot see it clearly. That is why it is vital to have other godly people in your life to help you clearly see things when you cannot. It is not weakness on your part; you are just too close. We should welcome, and even invite, the perspective and wisdom of other godly people in our lives.

Over and over, we see Ruth going to Naomi for instruction and direction. Through Ruth's submission to the guidance of Naomi, we see her walk straight into God's purpose and destiny for her!

### 3⟩ Ruth received favor from God. (Ruth 2:10)

Ruth didn't deserve the favor she received. She was a foreigner and was supposed to receive anything but favor. Because she associated with and clung to Naomi, the favor Naomi received carried to Ruth as well.

Ruth did not expect or deserve this God-given favor, but she received it humbly as a daughter.

### 4⟩ Ruth was a woman of noble character. (Ruth 2:11-12)

As a daughter, Ruth carried a heart of obedience and a heart of virtue. (Ruth 3:10) In Ruth 3:11, Boaz states *"all of the townsmen know that you are a woman of noble character."* Ruth's reputation of godly character had spread throughout Bethlehem. It was because Ruth stayed close to Naomi that she learned this godly character. Naomi's reputation became Ruth's reputation simply because Ruth positioned herself close to a woman who loved God and whose reputation was proof of that love.

I Corinthians 15:33 tells us, *"Do not be misled: Bad company corrupts good character"*. Your character can become corrupted and your reputation ruined by the company you keep. A wise woman will choose Godly company to keep so that her good character can remain as a testimony to others. Believe me, others are watching!

### 5) Ruth had a teachable heart and listened to Godly counsel. (Ruth 2:22-23)

Ruth continued to obey the direction that Naomi gave her. Remember, for Naomi, this was her homeland; she knew the ways and customs of this land. Ruth did not. Over and over again we see Ruth remaining teachable in her own heart and saying to Naomi, *"I'll do whatever you say."* (Ruth 3:5)

As a daughter, you have a choice in whether you have a teachable heart or not. Ruth had that same choice. We must remember that other people have walked before us and have more insight and wisdom than we do. We cannot have a "know it all" attitude. We should not only have an open, teachable heart, but we should also invite the wisdom and counsel of others into our lives.

## 6⟩ Ruth left a legacy.

Because of Ruth's determination to follow her mother-in-law into an unknown land, all of eternity was forever changed!

Out of one selfless decision, Ruth placed herself in the position for God to use her to change the course of history by becoming part of the lineage of His Son, Jesus.

At the time, Ruth had no idea what her choices, decisions, and intent of her heart would lead to, but God did. We will probably never know what our eternal impact on this earth will be until we get to heaven and see how it all unfolds. Our responsibility is to continue to carry a teachable, submitted, obedient heart just like Ruth.

## 7⟩ Ruth's blessings in turn blessed Naomi. (Ruth 4:13-17)

When Ruth was blessed with a son, she in turn blessed Naomi as if she had had a son herself. As daughters, we are to always bless the Naomi's who have gone before us! There have been countless women who have forged a difficult road in order for us to walk freely down that same road. We are to honor and esteem those women who have walked before us. Without them, we would not be receiving the blessings or favor God has so graciously given us.

**CHAPTER 8**

1. Would you consider yourself a Ruth, a Naomi, or both? Explain.

2. Who are some of the Ruth relationships in your life? Women who look to you for guidance, counsel, and wisdom?

3. What women do you consider as the Naomis in your life?

4. Give your definition of submission.

5. What relationships in your life are you submitted to? Have you made it easy for them to speak truth to you? If not, why not?

6. Tell of a situation you walked through when you could not clearly see the path ahead of you and how the relationships in your life helped you see a clearer perspective. How did their perspective change the way you walked through that season?

7. Would you say that you have a teachable heart? Would others say the same of you?

8. Specifically, how can you have a more teachable heart?

*chapter nine*

# Changing Your Name

*Ruth 1:19-22*

*So the two women went on until they came to Bethlehem. When they arrived in Bethlehem, the whole town was stirred because of them, and the women exclaimed, "Can this be Naomi?" "Don't call me Naomi," she told them. "Call me Mara, because the Almighty has made my life very bitter. I went away full, but the Lord has brought me back empty. Why call me Naomi? The Lord has afflicted me; the Almighty has brought misfortune upon me." So Naomi returned from Moab accompanied by Ruth the Moabite, her daughter-in-law, arriving in Bethlehem as the barley harvest was beginning.*

$I$ can't imagine what Naomi (or Ruth for that matter) must have been feeling as she returned to her homeland and her people. The Bible tells us that "the whole town was stirred because of them," and the women of Bethlehem exclaimed, *"Can this be Naomi?"*. It had been over ten years since this family had left Bethlehem. A lot had happened in Naomi's life over those ten long years.

Women have this sixth sense called "women's intuition", and it's a real thing. We just know when something is wrong. Whether it be with one of our children, our spouse, a family member, or friend, when something is wrong, WE JUST KNOW IT. Now don't ask us how we know, we just do. It's a gift we have, and 99.999999% of the time, we are right. ☺ Even after not seeing Naomi for more than ten years, the women in Bethlehem, Naomi's friends and relatives, knew something was not quite right with her. They just knew. In those days there was little means of communication, so it is highly improbable that these women knew of the hardships that Naomi had faced. Now she was returning home, and she was returning with a foreign girl, no one else. Not her husband nor her sons. Just Ruth.

In verses 20 and 21, Naomi doesn't give the women a chance to guess what's wrong with her. She declares it for all to hear. I like Naomi just boldly declaring her issues! She tells these women, *"Don't call me Naomi. Call me Mara because the Almighty has made my life very bitter. I went away full, but the Lord has brought me back empty. Why call me Naomi? The Lord has afflicted me; the Almighty has brought misfortune upon me."* WOW! No need for interpretation or opinions in deciding what was wrong with Naomi. She laid out very clearly what she had become over the ten years in Moab, and unfortunately, she blamed God.

That's what bitter women do. They blame God and others for the suffering that has happened to them.

Naomi's name means "pleasant one". She was once known for her pleasantness, as her name states. She had walked through some very tragic times and renamed herself "Mara", which means "bitter". Perhaps that is why the whole town of Bethlehem was in an uproar. The once pleasant Naomi was returning home after a decade, but she didn't look or sound like the same Naomi they had known before. The woman that returned was no longer pleasant, but bitter. Very bitter. So bitter, in fact, that she changed her name to reflect her now bitter heart.

In Naomi's explanation of her new name and disposition, she explains it this way: *"I went away full but the Lord has brought me back empty"* (v.21). There is a long way from being completely full to completely empty! You have to drive your car a long way for the gas tank dial to move from FULL to EMPTY.

**What happened to Naomi between full and empty?**
**Life happened. Suffering happened. Loss happened.**

The once "pleasant one" had traveled the road of pain and heartbreak, and that road led her to become the "bitter" one. Through her circumstances, Naomi had allowed a "root of bitterness" to grow within her heart.

Hebrews 12:15 tells us what can happen if we allow bitterness to take root in our hearts. It says, *"See to it that no one misses the grace of God and that no bitter root grows up to cause trouble and defile many."* By al-

lowing bitterness to take root in our hearts, WE MISS OUT ON THE GRACE OF GOD. I don't know about you, but I am desperate for God's grace. I'm not willing to allow a circumstance, a person, or a difficult season in my life to cause me to miss out on the grace of God! A bitter root in our hearts will also cause us a lot of trouble and will defile (taint, or make unclean) the relationships in our lives. Allowing bitterness to take root in our hearts is just not worth it!

We don't go to bed one night as the "pleasant one" and wake up the next morning as the "bitter one". A lot has to happen in our hearts between those two things. I love the way TD Jakes describes bitterness: "Bitterness really comes from failure to handle strong, negative emotions properly." We all will have times of feeling strong, negative emotions. Anger, jealously, hurt, pride, unforgiveness, fear, etc. are emotions that we have all felt and will continue to feel over our lifetimes because we live in a fallen, sinful world with fallen, sinful people - including ourselves. It is what we do with those negative emotions (or don't do with them) that determines whether or not a root of bitterness will grow within our hearts.

That is why the Bible commands us to *"guard our hearts above all else"* (Proverbs 4:23). Our hearts are where those negative emotions and feelings go to fester and grow if we are not guarding it. Slowly but surely, as time goes by, unforgiveness, wounds, pains, hurts, and suffering will grow into a root of bitterness if left unattended to. That's exactly what happened to Naomi. She even changed her name to protect herself from any expectations her people may have had of her to be the "pleasant one". That's a serious root of bitterness.

Have you allowed hardships in your life to change your name? Maybe not outwardly for all to hear like Naomi, but inwardly? Your once pleasant, joyful, loving personality and disposition is just a distant memory after the seasons of life you've walked through. Have you allowed a painful, difficult circumstance to change who you really are and were created by God to be? By doing so, you run very low on the grace of God, which means you don't have grace for anyone, including yourself.

This is what I find so hopeful and amazing: Naomi is the only person that called herself "Mara" or bitter. No one else called or named her that; God didn't, and no one else in Bethlehem did either. Only Naomi.

**Whatever "name" you've allowed to settle on you through your painful seasons, you're the only one who put it there. NO ONE ELSE IS CALLING YOU THAT NAME. Most certainly, not God.**

He named you for who He created you to be and the purposes within you. The "name" He's placed on you while you were still in your mother's womb (Psalm 139:13) is the same name that has remained on you throughout your life, throughout your hardships and pain. Only you have allowed that "name" to change.

The good news is this: If you are the only one who has placed that "name" on you, then you are the only one who can remove that "name" *from* you. You have the power within your own heart and soul to get that "name" off of you. You even have the power to re-move the "name" that others may have placed on you: an ex husband or boyfriend, a bitter mother, an abusive father, or a friend who be-trayed you. Whatever "name" they have called you is not the name that God has placed on you! You are a daughter of the Most High King! You are the apple of God's eye, and He is the Maker of Heaven and Earth! You have a purpose and destiny created for you before you were ever born, and though seasons and circumstances may have gotten you off the road to your purpose, it's never too late to "set out on the road that will take you back home". It is possible. No matter how long of a life you've lived, or how far off the road you have veered, or how many mistakes you've made, a road home has been prepared for you and so has a new name. Just look at Naomi.

# discussion questions

1. Describe a time when your woman's "intuition" kicked in. Did your intuition prove to be true? Explain.

2. What emotions do you feel as you return home for a visit with family and friends? Are they positive or negative emotions? Why?

3. What "names" have you allowed to be placed on you because of a specific season you have walked through? Did you place those names on yourself, or did someone else? Explain.

4. In your life experience, what does a bitter woman look like? Behave like?

5. Have you allowed hardships in your life to change your name? How so?

6. Share a time in your life when you experienced GRACE, either from others or from God, or both.

7. How does it feel to receive grace from God? How does it make you feel when you freely give grace to others?

8. Take a moment to either journal and/or pray, asking God to show you a "name" that may have been placed on you as a result of a difficult season you've walked through. Remove that "name" off of you by releasing it to God, making a choice not to be identified as that "name" any longer. Then express your gratitude to God for that release.

# The Deadly Root of Bitterness

*Ruth 1:20*
*"Call me Mara, because the Almighty has made my life*
*very bitter."*

*a* bitter heart can be very damaging. Not only to yourself and your own heart, but also to the hearts of others as well.

I know what a bitter woman looks like. Had I left my heart "unguarded" all those years, I would have become a bitter woman myself. Bitterness can rip lives apart. It can rip apart families, hearts, dreams, and what could have been. Trust me, I know.

Here are some similar characteristics that most bitter women have. I see these in Naomi's life and in my own personal experiences with other women.

## 1) **A bitter woman will blame God for her suffering.**

In verse 20, Naomi declares *"the Almighty has made my life bitter"*. Naomi blamed the very One whom had been so close to her and gave her the strength and courage to get back on her road home. She blamed the One whose hand protected and guarded her during her darkest days. He was now the One whom Naomi blamed for all her hardships and suffering.

Please don't blame God for your times of suffering. When we blame God, it creates a wedge between us and the One whom we think caused our hardship. We retreat and withdraw from Him, and we wake up one day, far from God and full of bitterness. Allow your suffering to draw you close to the One who knows and understands your pain more than anyone else.

### $2$ A bitter woman will not allow people close to her, and as a result will complain that she is alone.

Naomi wasn't drawing close to the women in Bethlehem: the ones who knew and loved her most. She explained to them why she was not the same woman they remembered.

I've often heard it said, "Hurt people, hurt people". No truer words have been spoken. People who are hurt will hurt other people and most often the people closest to them. Then they will complain when the ones they love most retreat from them because they cannot withstand the hurt and pain anymore.

A bitter woman doesn't want anyone close to her. The closer people get to her, the greater the chance they will see her heart and speak truth to the areas that she doesn't want to hear about.

### 3) A bitter woman will make it hard for others to love them.

It's hard to love a bitter woman. A bitter woman keeps everyone at arms length because she doesn't want to get hurt again. She views everyone that comes into her life through the lens of her pain and bitterness. Until she comes to the realization that bitterness has taken root and she needs the loving hand of God to come remove it from her heart, no one really stands a chance of penetrating her heart, not even God. And He will. She just has to recognize it and ask Him.

### 4) A bitter woman has allowed her heart to become hardened.

Proverbs 4:23 tells us to *"guard"* our hearts, not harden. A guarded heart protects from negative emotions and feelings from sticking to it. A hardened heart has walls built around it, daring anyone to come close. A guarded heart brings the "issues" to God, allowing Him to touch and heal those painful places. A hardened heart harbors the "issues", dwells on them, and eventually allows those untended areas of pain to grow into a root of bitterness.

Guarding our hearts is a continual process. We should never stop guarding our hearts. By doing so, you allow the grace of God to continue to flow through your life.

### 5) A bitter woman is often the most hurtful to the people closest to her.

Naomi tried to push away the two girls that she loved the most and who loved her in return. A bitter woman can put on a mask in front of a lot of people in her life to cover up her bitterness. The ones closest to her can clearly see her bitterness of heart. Naomi had become so consumed with her bitterness that an entire town saw it. You can only hide bitterness for so long. It first spills out to the people closest to you, then it eventually spills out for everyone to see.

### 6) A bitter woman is very self-centered.

Everything is always about HER! Her feelings, the wrongs that have happened to her, the pain that other people have brought to her, etc.

Naomi never once recognized or validated the hardships that Ruth would be facing. Naomi was going home. Home to her people, her family, her customs, and her God. Ruth was going to a foreign land, a different culture, no family, no relationships, and no promise of a blessed future. Naomi couldn't see what Ruth was walking into because all she could see at that moment was what was happening to her.

### 7) A bitter woman doesn't see her responsibility for her shortcomings. She only sees the mistakes in others.

A bitter woman is blinded by her own bitterness. That is why it is so

important to have other people in our lives to help us see what we cannot see in ourselves. We need people in our lives that can speak truth to us, even if it hurts: good friends, a pastor or leader, and family members that can see objectively.

A bitter woman must take responsibility for her own heart and what she's allowed to take root in it, but she must also invite and be open to the counsel and truth from those people who know her best and love her the most. If not, the root of bitterness will continue to grow.

If there's something within your own heart that you cannot shake or something you continue to deal with over and over, seek the counsel of others. Set up an appointment with a Christian counselor, a pastor, or a trusted Godly friend who can speak the truth to you in love, and then be prepared to receive the truth that is spoken. Don't make excuses or blame other people. Just hear and receive the truth and allow God to begin to touch and heal those areas of your heart. Your healing will take time and much effort on your part to allow Him to bring the healing you need. It's so worth it in the end. Bitterness can be removed and healed from your heart, but you are the only one who can take the first step towards your healing.

### 8 ) A bitter woman will isolate herself and will refuse the help of others.

Naomi begged Ruth and Orpah to stay in Moab. She wanted to return to Bethlehem alone, in her bitterness of heart. Thank God for a determined daughter-in-law!

The enemy's strategy has always been to "isolate and destroy." His plan is to isolate you, so that he can eventually destroy you. Not physically destroy you but destroy the purposes and plans that God has for your life. He wants to destroy you mentally and emotionally to where you cannot hear words of truth and affirmation that God speaks over you. If the enemy can keep you isolated, he can keep you defeated and deceived.

Do not allow the enemy to isolate you! Purposefully reach out and connect to godly people in your life. Stay relationally connected to your church family. There is strength in numbers, and when you're at the end of your own strength, draw from the strength of the people God has placed in your life.

It takes humility to allow other people to get close enough to you to help. Bitterness loses ground in our hearts when we choose to walk in humility and accept the help and counsel of others.

More often than not, your total healing of your heart will come not only from God Himself, but also through the people He's divinely brought into your life.

## 9⟩ A bitter woman turns into someone she's really not.

I have seen this with my own eyes (far too many times!) not only

within my own family, but also in the lives of women I've had the privilege and honor of pastoring for the past twenty-seven years. A bitter woman doesn't intend to turn into a bitter woman. It happens slowly over time for all the reasons I previously stated.

A once happy and joyful woman becomes depressed. A once social, life of the party woman becomes isolated. A once caring and compassionate woman becomes hard-hearted and self-centered. The list goes on and on.

A bitter heart can ruin your life and the lives of your family and friends.

My own mother was a wonderful woman and mother. She loved her family. She did the best she could do with what she had. She chose a different life for her family than what had been given to her. But as the years went by and the issues of her own heart were left untended to, bitterness began to grow, and she began to turn into a woman that we didn't even know. We all watched it happened, and it was heartbreaking. She allowed bitterness to turn her into a different person. A lack of joy, confidence, grace, peace, and love became evident in the life of my mother, and the "abundant" life that is promised to us was all but robbed from her. It has been sad to watch, even from a distance.

Please don't allow bitterness to remain in your heart. It will turn you into someone you never intended to be, and you will find yourself alone.

## 10 ` A bitter mother can raise bitter children.

Just like alcoholics or drug addicts can raise children who deal with the same addictions, a bitter mother can raise bitter sons and daughters. Ironically, the sons' and daughters' bitterness is usually towards their bitter mother!

I have wrestled with bitterness in my own heart toward my mother. Had I not allowed, and continue to allow, God to address and touch that area in my heart, I would have become the very thing that I've hated seeing in my mother: a bitter woman. I do not hate my mother. I just hate what she has turned into and the pain she has brought to herself and our family.

If you're a daughter of a bitter mother, please hear my heart. You have no idea the journey that your mother has walked or the upbringing she had. You don't know the abuse she may have suffered or the heartbreak and pain she may have had to endure. Her intent has never been to bring hurt, suffering, or distance to you, her daughter. She would tell you that if she knew how. You have to give grace to your mother. You have not walked in her shoes or carried the issues she has in her heart. What she's done to you or how she's treated you may be inexcusable, but it is not unforgiveable. Nothing is unforgiveable. We, as daughters, have been forgiven much, and we are commanded by God to forgive others. Period. That doesn't mean forgiveness is easy or comes quickly, because it doesn't. It takes time, and it is a process. You at least have to recognize the necessity of forgiveness towards your mother and be moving in that direction.

**Forgiving your mother (or anyone else for that matter) doesn't make what she's done RIGHT. It just makes you FREE.**

In order for you to be free from unforgiveness and bitterness, you have to forgive her.

As a daughter, you also need to come to the realization that you are probably not the person that is going to bring this truth to your mother. You are just too close. You need to pray that God will send people to your mother that she will listen to and receive truth from and then allow God to work in her heart. You stay out of it and work on guarding your own heart. God is perfectly capable and willing to work on your mother's heart. Prayerfully, she'll receive the healing of her heart that God desires for her, and you and your mother's relationship can be healed as well. If not, you receive the healing for your own heart and don't allow your hurt to hurt other people.
Release her and your pain to God.

It is my sole responsibility to guard my own heart from bitterness. No one else is responsible for my heart but me. The same is true for you. You may have walked through terrible tragedy and pain in your life, and none of those circumstances may be your fault. You are responsible for whatever you allow to remain in your heart and grow there. Verse 22 says, *"so Naomi returned…"* She left Moab and returned back to the promised land of God. Even in her bitterness of heart, Naomi knew the right place to go…home to Bethlehem. Back to the "house of bread and praise" God had for her. Back to the place of provision and Presence where she belonged.

A final thought on bitterness:

In Ruth chapter 2, everything seemed to change once Naomi realized she was needed again. Not only did she have a reason to live, she now also had a purpose…Ruth.

Any person who is bitter will benefit from helping others because they have the opportunity to focus on something other than themselves.

If you have found yourself with a root of bitterness in your heart, place that bitter root in the hand of God, NOT in your heart!

Naomi's bitterness was turned into blessing. Her sadness turned into joy, and her empty heart, soul, and life were filled and restored.

Eventually, Naomi made a choice that all survivors make. SHE CHOSE TO LIVE ON! Somewhere between chapter 1 and chapter 2 of Ruth, Naomi got up and decided to live her life WITHOUT HER BITTERNESS!  And so can you!

# CHAPTER 10
## discussion questions

1.  Do you have women in your family who are bitter? Are you a woman with bitterness in your heart?

2.  Of those characteristics of a bitter woman described in chapter 10, which ones are most true of you? Explain.

3.  Have you seen the bitterness in your heart before now? If not, why not?

4.  After reading chapter 10, what is the revelation of bitterness that you feel God has shown you?

5.  What are some specific things God is asking of you so that bitterness does not remain in your heart? Are you willing to do those things?

6.  Either within your small group or with a trusted friend or leader, share your experience with bitterness and have a time of prayer releasing that bitterness to God.

# *chapter eleven*

# This Isn't What I Expected

*"God has a beautiful way of bringing good
vibrations out of broken chords."*
*- Charles Swindoll*

The last verse of Ruth chapter 1 says, *"So Naomi returned from Moab accompanied by Ruth the Moabitess, her daughter in law, arriving in Bethlehem as the barley harvest was beginning."* (v.22)

Before we dive into chapter 2 of Ruth, I wonder what Ruth must have been thinking as she and Naomi arrived in Bethlehem? This was a new country to Ruth: a new culture, a new people, a new way of life, and a new God, Whose Hand she would soon see in her life.

Between the end of chapter 1 and the beginning of chapter 2, what was Ruth's mood and mindset? Was it anticipation and excitement? Nervousness, anxiety, or fear of the unknown? Or could it have been disappointment? Disappointment of what was supposed to be - dreams of a happy life and family in her own country of Moab?

I heard a speaker make the following statement when speaking about adoption: "It's not what I expected, but it's what I have". I think that statement is also true in terms of our families and their dynamics. I know it's true of mine. For far too long, I wrestled with the expectation of the way things were supposed to be. I held tightly to that expectation, trying again, so hard, to fix and mend the brokenness in my extended family.

"A healthy family should look like this…"

"A healthy family should do this…"

"A healthy family behaves like this…"

On and on my thoughts and expectations would go, only to be left disappointed over and over again.

I finally came to the realization that my expectations were unrealistic. My "healthy family" ideals were not happening, and most likely, would never be happening. I had to let go. Let go of the unrealistic expectations I had set up in my mind of the way things were "supposed to be". The more expectations I had, the more let down and disappointed I had become. My expectations were unrealistic. It simply was not going to happen as I had long envisioned and hoped.

I am certainly not saying to let go of your hope, faith, and belief that God will intervene in your situation. I am not saying to stop praying. Absolutely not! I am saying, however, that we must release the EXPECTATION of how we think that prayer should be answered, how that person needs to change, or how a circumstance needs to be different in our lives. Our expectations and the reality of what God knows to be best for us can be two totally different things.

"This is not what I expected, but it is what I have." A broken, fragmented family. While I had no control over how family members behaved or acted towards me, I did have control over my response to those actions and words. I did have control over whether I would continue to place myself in a situation or environment in which hurt would surely come. Once I understood that, I could release my unrealistic expectations to God and be released from the ideal of how things were supposed to be.

The situation didn't change. The brokenness didn't change. People didn't change, but I changed. I was now free from the heavy weight of unrealistic expectations of my broken family, and I left them in the hands of God. He could change them. I could not. (God knows I tried!)

I removed myself from the drama of my family. I did not engage in negative conversations about their drama. I refused to be pulled in. THAT I could control. That was when the weight lifted from my shoulders and I became FREE.

There are so many things in life that you simply have no control over whatsoever. Let those things (and people) go. You do have control over YOU. Who you choose to associate with, where you choose to go, what drama you choose to be a part of, which conversations you allow yourself to engage in.

**You can control what you have the power to control, and that's YOU.**

Here is a warning: not everyone is going to understand that. And that is okay. You are in charge of YOU...period.

You do not have to stay in the back seat of the bus of family drama. When you are in the backseat, wherever that bus goes, you also go with no say so as to where the bus is going or who it's picking up along the way. Move yourself to the front seat of the bus, allowing yourself to choose what you need to be a part of. You even have the ability to get off of the bus too. Some family buses are going down a road that you have no business going down. The end of the road leads to destruction and pain. For some, you may need to get off the bus before it crashes and takes you with it.

Trust me, you can still get off the bus and do so with honor, respect, and love for your family members. This is solely determined by the posture of your heart. Guilt keeps you on a bus that's headed for destruction.

I don't know what Ruth was feeling or thinking as she and Naomi walked out of chapter 1 and into chapter 2. Maybe she had some unrealistic expectations to release also. Just maybe, she also felt the freedom from the weight as she entered into the city of Bethlehem.

What expectations in your own heart do you need to release? Why not take some time and give those expectations to God? Let Him know that you trust Him to answer that prayer and intervene in that situation for your best good. Be prepared. The answer may not look like you had envisioned. You can trust Him that it will be good because He is a good God who only does good for His children. (Psalm 119: 68)

Release the expectation, the person, the situation, the weight, and the burden you have been carrying to God. Hold nothing back. His shoulders can withstand what is crushing yours. He can carry it. I promise!

# CHAPTER 11

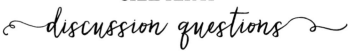

*discussion questions*

1. Have you ever had an expectation that didn't turn out as you thought it would? Explain.

2. Describe the feelings you had when that expectation did not become a reality.

3. What expectations do you have concerning your extended family? Are they realistic or unrealistic?

4. What expectations in your own heart do you need to release? Take some time in prayer to release those expectations to God.

5. As you release your expectations, it places you in a greater position to trust God. Do you honestly and wholeheartedly trust Him with your prayers? What's keeping you from trusting Him completely?

# Initiative vs. Entitlement

*Ruth 2:1-3*

*Now Naomi had a relative on her husband's side, a man
of standing from the clan of Elimelech, whose name was
Boaz. And Ruth the Moabite said to Naomi, "Let me go
to the fields and pick up the leftover grain behind anyone
in whose eyes I find favor." Naomi said to her, "Go ahead,
my daughter." So she went out, entered a field and began
to glean behind the harvesters.*

*A*s we move into chapter 2 of Ruth, there is a bit of a shift in
characters. Naomi takes a back seat, and we are introduced to a man
named Boaz. Naomi is still an important part of this story, but the
focus turns to Ruth and Boaz.

Boaz's name means "in him is strength," and as we learn more about him, we see how he certainly lives up to his name. The first verse tells us how Boaz was a relative to Naomi, which becomes very significant as the story of this family continues to unfold.

Soon after arriving in Bethlehem, Ruth asks Naomi to allow her to "go into the fields and pick up leftover grain." In that simple request, we see a characteristic in Ruth that, sadly, isn't very common today, especially among our youth. The characteristic is INITIATIVE.

Ruth took initiative and didn't wait on Naomi to provide for her. Bethlehem was Naomi's hometown, a place she was very familiar with, but Ruth was not. That didn't deter Ruth one bit. Ruth quickly realized that, as two widows now having to provide for themselves, she needed to do something, and she took initiative to do just that. Ruth went into the fields to work, to gather grain that was left behind from the harvesters.

Webster's definition of initiative is "the readiness and ability to take action; an introductory (beginning) step or action." My definition of initiative is "to get up and do something; not waiting on someone else to do what you need to do". Now, you choose which definition is more gracious.

Ruth could have sat in Naomi's home and prayed to God for Him to provide food for them. She could have gathered the Bethlehem women's prayer group to pray and fast for their provision, but she didn't. Ruth got up and did something. She took initiative. Because of Ruth's initiative, her get up and go, her step of action, God blessed her move.

She found herself in the field of a man named Boaz.

Too often in our Christian worlds, we can use prayer as an excuse not to take action. Is prayer important? ABSOLUTELY! Is prayer vital to our walk with God? WITHOUT A DOUBT! Can we pray and ask God to meet our needs? OF COURSE WE CAN, and we should, but far too often all we do is pray and do nothing else. There are instances where all we can do is pray. Our circumstances are beyond our control and prayer is the only posture and action we have, on our knees before God. There are many other instances where prayer should be our starting point, and after the "amen" to our prayers, we should get up and take a step of action and faith in doing our part to see the needs met in our lives and the lives of those we love.

Because of Ruth's initiative in doing whatever was necessary to provide for Naomi and herself, God honored and blessed her. He allowed the eye of Boaz to fall upon a hard working, honest, humble girl with great initiative and character. Verse 3 tells us, "she went out and began to glean in the fields behind the harvesters." Before you can see the significance of Ruth's action, you have to first understand the what and why of gleaning. In Bible times, God's law made a provision for the widows and poor through gleaning. The Israelite law declared that the workers harvesting the fields were to leave the corners of the field for the gleaners, and anything that was dropped during harvesting had to be left for them (Leviticus 19:9, 23:22, Deuteronomy 24:19).

This law would be equivalent to our modern day welfare programs.

The initiative that Ruth took to get provision for herself and Naomi is something that today is hard to find. The opposite characteristic of initiative is entitlement. Dr. John Townsend, in his book <u>The Entitlement Cure</u>, describes entitlement as "the belief that I am exempt from responsibility but am owed special treatment." There was not an entitled bone in Ruth's body. Today, through government programs that are intended to provide and care for those less fortunate or those going through seasons of financial hardship, we find ourselves facing a generation of people that have become entitled to financial help and provision. We are surrounded by a generation of people that expect the help instead of working for or appreciating the help for just a season until they get back on their feet.

Ruth was not embarrassed or too prideful to go to the fields and glean behind the harvesters. Simply by being in the corners of the field, picking up the leftover grain, everyone knew that Ruth was either poor or widowed, or both. Ruth was not entitled, nor did she expect or demand the help provided to her in any way. What a different world we live in today!

We are raising a generation of young people who have been given everything they could ever want or ask for, without the responsibility of working for that privilege. We as mothers have done and provided everything our children wish for, and in doing so, we have done a great disservice to them and to our communities. We now have a generation of young people who have no work ethic and no initiative. They graduate high school or college and go out into the work force, not knowing how to work hard and keep a job, and employers are at a loss. Just ask any business owner or employer you know. Most will say the same thing: "Good, honest, dependable, hard working employees are almost impossible to find".

Entitlement has replaced initiative. Laziness, lack of taking responsibility and an expectation of special treatment have replaced hard work, humility, and gratitude. Dishonesty has replaced good, old-fashioned honesty and integrity. An unrealistic expectation of starting at the top rung of the ladder has replaced starting at the bottom and working hard to move to the top rung. Our communities and country are suffering because of this mindset.

Mamas, please listen to me and hear my heart: stop doing everything for your children! In doing so, you are not teaching them initiative. Stop fighting their battles. Stop interfering in every aspect of their lives. Stop taking their side with teachers, principals, law enforcement, etc. unless it is legitimate. Teach them to respect authority. Allow your children and teens to feel the repercussions of their choices. Stop rescuing them. Stop hovering over them. Allow children to play and work out their own differences. Allow them to fail at times. Teach them how to get back up every time they fall, both literally and figuratively. Teach them how to work hard for a privilege they want. Make them get a job when they are of age. Expect them to carry some of the responsibility within your home through chores and daily to-do lists. Stop going behind them and cleaning up their messes...again, both literally and figuratively.

**We are raising a generation of young people to go out into this world to make a God-difference, but this world isn't going to go easy on them. Neither should you.**

Teach them responsibility, hard work, humility, loyalty, and initiative now, while they are in your home, so they can learn and even fail in a safe, loving environment. In doing so, you can help them navigate the lessons of life while they are with you. If not, they will learn the lessons the hard way, away from you, out in the world on their own. I promise you, the world won't be nearly as gracious and forgiving to them as you will be. Please take your God-given assignment of parenting seriously. A better community and a better world depends on it. Parenting is the hardest job on the planet, but it also bears the greatest rewards. One day, your children and society will thank you for it!

Because of Ruth's initiative, God brought His blessings to her. He provided for her not only in that moment but for the remainder of her life, simply because of her initiative of obedience, carrying no expectation of special treatment. The same will be true of you and your children. Do not offer the easy road to your children, absent of responsibility. God doesn't offer the easy road to you or to them.

# CHAPTER 12
## discussion questions

**1.** What would be your definition of initiative? Of entitlement? Describe in your own words the difference between those two characteristics.

**2.** Why do you think we see such a lack of initiative in our younger generation? What things have contributed to that lack?

**3.** Do you struggle with showing initiative? Why? Do your children struggle with initiative? How might have you contributed to their lack of initiative?

**4.** Explain about a time when you took initiative in a particular situation. What was the outcome of your initiative?

**5.** What are some specific ways you see entitlement in our current society?

**6.** Do you feel entitled in an area of your life? Why or why not?

**7.** As adults, in your opinion, how can we better equip the next generation to develop the characteristic of initiative, not the characteristic of entitlement?

# A Just so Happened Moment

*Ruth 2:3*
*And she just happened to stop at the part of the field belonging to Boaz, who was of the family of Elimelech.*

The NIV version of Ruth 2:3 tells us *"As it turned out, she found herself working in a field belonging to Boaz, who was from the clan of Elimelech."* The Amplified version says, "She *happened* to stop…" If we just began reading in Chapter 2 of Ruth, it would look like Ruth was in the right place at the right time. It would seem that, perhaps, luck or coincidence would have her in Boaz's field. But it wasn't the luck of Ruth or a coincidence. It was her decision back in chapter 1 to stay with Naomi and to *"go wherever she goes"* that led Ruth to her "just so happened moment".

**RUTH DID NOT CHOOSE THE RIGHT FIELD,
SHE CHOSE THE RIGHT PERSON.
IT WAS THE RIGHT PERSON THAT LED HER
TO THE RIGHT FIELD.**

There are no "just so happened" moments in God's plans. He is the Good Shepherd who promises to lead and guide His children into *"paths of righteousness"* (Psalm 23:3 ESV), and our own right choices will lead us to our "just so happened moments" in life.

Our purpose and destiny in God is always linked and connected to other people. God brings other people into our lives, many times through divine circumstances, to lead and guide us straight to His plan for our lives. An old wise pastor once told my husband and I, "The kingdom of God is built on relationships." No truer words have ever been spoken. Ecclesiastes 4:9-10 confirms that, *"Two are better than one, because they have a good return for their work: If one falls down, his friend can help him up. But pity the man who falls and has no one to help him up!"*

Looking back over my life, Godly relationships have been what have led me to my "just so happened moments" and, ultimately, to God's purpose and plan for my life. After walking into a new church when I was thirteen years old, I became divinely connected with the pastor and his family who ultimately became like family to me.

It was my pastor and his family that cultivated in me a heart for ministry and a love for God's church. It was this same family that was hugely influential in what bible college I would attend. It would be at that bible college that I would meet my husband. It would be through relationships that led my future husband (and eventually myself, after we married) to our very first ministry position in New Orleans, Louisiana. For the next twenty-seven years, God-relationships are what led us down every road in ministry that God had laid out before us.

It was over thirty years ago through a divine relationship, with our pastors, Jacob and Michelle Aranza, that we were led back to Louisiana to help pastor and serve the campuses of Our Savior's Church.

None of my journey thus far has been by luck or by coincidence. It has been through making the decision to recognize the people that God has divinely placed in my life over the years and staying close to them. I've chosen to "cling" to these divine relationships, and by doing so, it has led me into "fields" I could not have ever imagined that I would have found myself in.

As a young wife and woman in ministry, I often felt like Ruth, a foreigner in a foreign land having no idea what I was to do. I knew I had God's calling on my life, but back all those years ago, women in public ministry alongside their husbands weren't as prevalent as they are today. It seemed as if every woman in ministry I tried to "cling" to, in hopes of them showing me what to do, kept me at arms length.

Looking back, I know it was nothing personal. I realize now that they didn't know their own purpose, much less how to help me determine mine.

I remember vividly one day, in much frustration, crying out to God and asking Him why He hadn't sent me a spiritual mother, a Naomi, to help me on my journey in ministry. God immediately spoke clearly, yet firmly to my heart: "Heidi, if you will become to other women what you so desperately need yourself, I will become to you all that you need in ministry. I will lead you and show you how to walk your calling and purpose out if you will commit to help other women learn to walk out their calling and purpose."

At that moment, everything changed in me: my attitude, my heart, and my perspective. I now had an assignment from God, and I spent from that day forward trying to fulfill the role of a spiritual mother for other women, not only in ministry but also in every aspect of their lives. I never want a woman to leave my company saying, "No one ever showed me what to do." I've spent my entire adult life, humbly showing women what to do as God has shown me. As I became obedient in my new assignment from God, not only was He faithful in showing me what to do, He was also faithful to give me many wonderful, godly women in my life to speak purpose, encouragement, wisdom, and grace to me. Many of those relational gifts were from a distance. I listened to every message and teaching I could get my hands on. I read books concerning leadership, ministry, marriage, parenting, etc. I watched women in ministry and in life from a distance, gleaning from their lives in what I should do and even in what

I shouldn't do. I will be forever grateful to God for those gifts, both those close to me, whom I knew personally and those whom I may never meet who unknowingly invested much into my life!

Because I recognized and honored those relationships that God brought to me by staying close to them, I ultimately found myself in the dead center of God's will for me. Discovering God's purposes and plans for my life would not have happened without those Godly relationships, and neither will that same discovery happen for you. Not until you begin to cling to the people that God has sent to you to help you navigate your own journey.

**Ruth didn't choose the right field. She chose the right person. It was the right person who led her to the right field.**

Before you find yourself in the right field, you have to first determine who the right people are in your life that have been sent by God to help you, to lead you, to direct you on your journey in life, and/or in ministry. Until you first recognize who those people are, your right field will be very difficult to find.

Boaz's field represented provision, protection, and purpose to Ruth. His field ultimately became the place where God would reveal His divine plan for Ruth and Boaz's life. But Ruth could not have received God's purpose and plan for her had she first not recognized who Naomi was to her and how God had divinely connected them to one another. The same is true for you and I. Our "fields" await us, but in between today and finding yourself in your field of provision, protection, and purpose, there are some relationships that you first must recognize, embrace, and cultivate.

Look up and begin to recognize those divine relationships. They are there, whether they are near and personal to you, or whether they are at a distance. There are people that God has equipped and purposed to help you. You have to first identify who those people are, then you have to cling to them. What does clinging look like? It looks like taking a great step of faith by asking for help and guidance. It's staying close to the people that are divinely placed in your life. It's asking questions and preparing your heart to receive their honest answers. It's not being offended when they tell you the truth. It's resourcing yourself with podcasts, books, blogs, or sermon messages from people you admire and wish to pattern your life after. It's not only listening to wise, Godly counsel but DOING IT. It's making the necessary changes in your life that need to be made. It's determining what to say yes to and what to say no to. It's clearly setting your eyes on your God-given purpose and boldly living a life that will help you get there.

Your Naomis are out there. They are just waiting for you to recognize them as such. You have to look and identify them, then cling to them ever so tightly. On the other side of that recognition and embrace, your "just so happened moments" await you, dear Ruth.

# CHAPTER 13
## discussion questions

1.   What are the names of the divine relationships that God has connected you with?

2.   Describe a time in your life, as you look back, that you experienced a "just so happened" moment.

3.   What were the results of that "just so happened" moment?

4.   Is that decision still playing out in your life today? If so, how?

5.   What "field" does God have you serving in?  Explain the decisions that brought you to that "field".

6.   Take some time this week to handwrite a note of thanks and appreciation to those divine relationships that God has given you.

*chapter*
*fourteen*

# The Glance of God

*Ruth 2:4-13*

*Just then Boaz arrived from Bethlehem and greeted the harvesters, "The Lord be with you!" "The Lord bless you!" they answered. Boaz asked the overseer of his harvesters, "Who does that young woman belong to?" The overseer replied, "She is the Moabite who came back from Moab with Naomi. She said, 'Please let me glean and gather among the sheaves behind the harvesters.' She came into the field and has remained here from morning till now, except for a short rest in the shelter."*

*So Boaz said to Ruth, "My daughter, listen to me. Don't go and glean in another field and don't go away from here. Stay here with the women who work for me. Watch the field where the men are harvesting, and follow along after the women. I have told the men not to lay a hand on you. And whenever you are thirsty, go and get a drink from the water jars the men have filled." At this, she bowed down with her face to the ground. She asked him, "Why*

*have I found such favor in your eyes that you notice me
—a foreigner?" Boaz replied, "I've been told all about
what you have done for your mother-in-law since the
death of your husband—how you left your father and
mother and your homeland and came to live with a people you did not know before. May the Lord repay you
for what you have done. May you be richly rewarded by
the Lord, the God of Israel, under whose wings you have
come to take refuge."*

*"May I continue to find favor in your eyes, my lord,"
she said. "You have put me at ease by speaking kindly to
your servant—though I do not have the standing of one
of your servants."*

*It's* amazing how clearly we can see the hand of God in our lives once we have walked through a season of trial or testing! Once we get on the other side of a season, or a trial, or a circumstance, we can look back and clearly see the hand of God moving on our behalf. More times than not, we don't see God's hand clearly moving forward. That is why it's called "faith". We walk forward in faith, trusting that His hand will be there to lead and guide us. Once we get to the other side, we look back and see how God moved in our situation greatly.

As we continue reading in Ruth, we see the hand of God moving in the life of Naomi and Ruth. We see His direction and guidance for them, even when they couldn't see it themselves. We also have the privilege of reading about the moment the eyes of Boaz first take notice of Ruth.

*Ruth 2:5-9*

*Boaz asked the overseer of his harvesters, "Who does that young woman belong to?" The overseer replied, "She is the Moabite who came back from Moab with Naomi. She said, 'Please let me glean and gather among the sheaves behind the harvesters.' She came into the field and has remained here from morning till now, except for a short rest in the shelter." So Boaz said to Ruth, "My daughter, listen to me. Don't go and glean in another field and don't go away from here. Stay here with the women who work for me. Watch the field where the men are harvesting, and follow along after the women. I have told the men not to lay a hand on you. And whenever you are thirsty, go and get a drink from the water jars the men have filled."*

These verses give us insight into the first interaction between Boaz and Ruth. As Ruth is working in the fields gleaning, Boaz takes notice of her and asks his workers, *"Whose young woman is that?"* (v.5) Not only does Boaz notice her, he gives her instruction not to glean in any other fields. He also instructed his workers not to touch her (protection) and provided water for her when she became thirsty (provision). (v. 8-9)

To you and I in this day and age, these instructions from Boaz may not seem like a big deal, but it was. It was a huge deal because gleaners were not treated with this amount of kindness. The attitude of wealthy landowners towards the gleaners was one of mere tolerance.

Gleaners would not expect to be spoken to by the landowner, much less welcomed in his field. Such personal attention was highly unusual preferential treatment.

What Ruth experienced at that moment through Boaz's attention and care for her was nothing other than the favor of God. It wasn't unusual that Boaz noticed her in his field among all the workers. Ruth was a foreigner and would have stood out from the others who were working. What was unusual was the favor that Boaz showed her.

Years ago, I read a definition of the favor of God that I've never forgotten because it is absolutely true: **"The favor of God is God doing for you what you could never do for yourself."** That was certainly the case with Ruth. She could have never dreamed of the favor that Boaz showed her, which was ultimately God's favor on her life. God's favor on our lives is undeserved and nothing short of the grace of God. Ruth didn't carry God's favor with pride and entitlement but with great humility and gratitude.

In verse 10, Ruth bows before Boaz after hearing all that he has offered her and states, *"Why have I found such favor in your eyes that you notice me a foreigner?"* Once again, we see clearly the heart of humility in Ruth. Not expectation or entitlement. No pitifulness or neediness. Just humility, gratitude, and recognition of God's favor on her life through a man named Boaz.

Don't ever think for a moment that God or people are not watching you in the fields that you are working. Whether it be in a secular job or in a ministry job, people and God are watching. They are watching your attitude, your work ethic, and your interaction with other employees. They see your heart and mindset towards your work, or the lack thereof. People and God take notice, whether you realize it or not. They are both watching. A good employee, a good worker, a good leader will always stand out and will cause people and God to notice them. Your heart and your motives will be seen, and if both are pure, you will be rewarded by both God and people.

In verses 11 and 12, Boaz says *"I have been told all about what you have done for your mother-in-law since the death of your husband, how you left your father and mother and your homeland and came to live with a people you did not know before. May the Lord repay you for what you have done. May you be richly rewarded by the Lord, the God of Israel, under whose wings you have come to take refuge."*

Not only had Boaz taken notice of Ruth working in the fields, but the people of Bethlehem were talking about all that Ruth had done in tending to and caring for Naomi. In arguably one of the most devastating seasons of Ruth's life, God had seen ALL that Ruth had done. People had seen it too. In moments where I am certain that Ruth felt that no one else was with her, in dire times of loneliness and despair, in some of the darkest days of her life, the eyes of God saw EVERYTHING. Ultimately the people around her saw it too.

That's what character is. It is who you are and what you do when no one else is watching. Your character (who you are) shines the brightest in the darkest of times. Whatever Ruth did and wherever she went, her character remained the same. True character doesn't change with different people or in different circumstances. The decisions we make in dark times that no one else knows about, God notices it, and He will bless it.

Boaz took notice of Ruth, and God will take notice of you if you remain true to Him and exemplify true Godly character, even in the worst of times.

When the time comes and God is ready to fulfill His promises and purposes in you, HE WILL FIND YOU. Regardless of the field you're in or it's obscurity, GOD CAN AND WILL FIND YOU.

He found David in a field tending to his father's sheep.
He found Mary in the tiny, unknown town of Nazareth.
He found Ruth gleaning in the field of Boaz.
He most certainly can find you.

**God is the Master at reaching people
in their fields of obscurity.**

As long as your hand is at the plow working diligently in all that He's placed in your hands to do, when it is time, HE WILL FIND YOU. All it will take is one glance, one notice from an employer, a pastor, a publisher, a Boaz to change the trajectory of your entire life. It won't be you making it happen. Just like it wasn't Ruth that made Boaz notice her. It was God that ultimately decided. IT WAS TIME.

We live in a day and age of self-promotion. Through the use of social media, we can promote ourselves, our message, and our products. The business (and even many ministry) gurus' advice is pretty much the same: build your platform, market your name, your brand, and all you have to offer. While I am certainly not anti-social media, I am grateful for modern technology and the way God can use it to reach people for His glory. I am, however, bothered by how easy it has become to promote ourselves and build our own platforms. Because of what is afforded to us through social media and technology, we have become professionals at opening our own doors of opportunity and promoting our own names all in the name of ministry and Jesus.

Jesus never asked us to build our own platforms, but He did ask us to build His kingdom (Matthew 16:18-19). When we determine in our hearts to build HIS kingdom and not our own, the eyes of God takes notice. God doesn't need our help fulfilling His purposes in us. He is quite capable of doing that entirely on His own. Just ask Ruth.

As Ruth made a decision to stay close to Naomi, and ultimately her God, she found "refuge under His wings". God's hands stretched over her. His provision, protection, and purpose came to her. His eyes turned toward her without Ruth making a way for herself, without Ruth building a name for herself, without promoting herself or expecting entitlement or special privileges to come to her. God did it for her...period. No other explanation. ONLY GOD.

I will take God's promotion for me over my promotion for myself any day.

How about you?

# CHAPTER 14

## discussion questions

1. Describe a time when it was difficult to see God working in your life, but as you look back, you can now clearly see His Hand moving.

2. Share your own definition of the favor of God.

3. Explain of a moment when you experienced the favor of God in your life and in the lives of your family.

4. Have you felt obscure or overlooked at times? How so?

5. Give an example of how God has promoted you, either in your workplace, your ministry, or even within your own circle of friends and family.

6. What door of opportunity are you asking God to open for you? Is your desire that He be glorified in that opportunity, or are you now realizing that it may be YOU wanting the recognition?

7. Take a moment to pray and ask God to help you keep your heart pure and humble as you patiently wait for the right God-opportunity to be opened for you.

# chapter fifteen

# A Hope that Anchors

*Ruth 2:14-23*

*At mealtime Boaz said to her, "Come over here. Have some bread and dip it in the wine vinegar." When she sat down with the harvesters, he offered her some roasted grain. She ate all she wanted and had some left over. As she got up to glean, Boaz gave orders to his men, "Let her gather among the sheaves and don't reprimand her. Even pull out some stalks for her from the bundles and leave them for her to pick up, and don't rebuke her." So Ruth gleaned in the field until evening. Then she threshed the barley she had gathered, and it amounted to about an ephah. She carried it back to town, and her mother-in-law saw how much she had gathered. Ruth also brought out and gave her what she had left over after she had eaten enough. Her mother-in-law asked her, "Where did you glean today? Where did you work? Blessed be the man who took notice of you!" Then Ruth told her mother-in-law about the one at whose place she had been working. "The name of the*

*man I worked with today is Boaz," she said. "The Lord*
*bless him!" Naomi said to her daughter-in-law. "He has*
*not stopped showing his kindness to the living and the*
*dead." She added, "That man is our close relative; he is one*
*of our kinsman-redeemers." Then Ruth the Moabite said,*
*"He even said to me, 'Stay with my workers until they*
*finish harvesting all my grain.'" Naomi said to Ruth her*
*daughter-in-law, "It will be good for you, my daughter, to*
*go with the women who work for him, because in someone*
*else's field you might be harmed." So Ruth stayed close*
*to the women of Boaz to glean until the barley and wheat*
*harvests were finished. And she lived with her mother-*
*in-law.*

*I* don't think there's a more attractive quality in a person than
humility. Sadly, humility is not something we see often in today's
world. Too many times the humble gets trampled by the proud. The
proud person is much more vocal than the humble person and de-
mands more attention. The world gives them the attention and the
accolades, but the world's attention is not what we're striving for. It's
the attention of God we long for, or at least it should be. Humility
poured out of Ruth's life and actions, and the attention and opportunities that came to her because of her humble heart were astounding.

In verses 14 through 16, Ruth continued to see God's favor in her life
through Boaz. Boaz took his act of kindness one step further when he

insisted that Ruth glean from the sheaves (a bunch of stalks of grain that are tied together after being cut). What made this act of kindness so significant was that gleaning among the sheaves was not allowed. The law stated that gleaners had to stay in the corners of the field (Deuteronomy 25:5-10), but Boaz told his workers to allow Ruth to glean among the already cut stalks of grain within the field and then ordered them to drop handfuls of barley, on purpose, so that Ruth would have more than enough provision.

Had Ruth not been humble enough to glean in the fields in the first place, she would have missed a God-opportunity that came as Boaz showed great favor toward her.

We must not miss the fact that a heart of humility will open doors of opportunity that would not have been opened otherwise. A humble heart can make up for a lack of talent or skill. Humility will attract opportunities for you, while pride will repel people and opportunities. Not only does pride repel people, it repels God too. James 4:6 tells us, *"God opposes the proud but He gives grace to the humble."* God will resist or stiff-arm those who carry a prideful heart. Not only will God resist the proud, so will people and their opportunities for you. Proud people don't attract people close to them; they repel people away from them even more importantly, they repel the gracious hand of God. Humble hearted people attract and draw people to themselves, but God also draws near to them and covers them with His grace. Never once do we see an ounce of pride in Ruth's heart. Only humility. It was beautiful on her and attracted not only opportunity to her but also attracted a man named Boaz.

I remember a time when I was in bible college and I needed a job badly. There was a program called the "college work-study program" where you could work on campus, and a majority of your paycheck would go toward your tuition, leaving a little bit extra for spending money. I applied for this program, and an opportunity came my way. There was an opening for a resident assistant in my girl's dormitory. I would be overseeing all the girls that lived on a particular hallway by enforcing rules, doing routine room checks, giving spiritual guidance to them, etc. As I was being interviewed by the director of the dormitory, her first question to me was, "Would you be willing to take oversight of the rooms in the basement?" This meant that I wouldn't be overseeing a particular floor of girls, but I would be overseeing all the rooms in the basement of our dormitory. My answer was an immediate "Yes!" I was desperate for a job. To my surprise, as soon as the director heard my enthusiastic "Yes!", I was hired immediately. No other questions asked.

The dorm director later told me the number one reason I had gotten the job was because I was willing to take the rooms in the basement. She went on to tell me that she had interviewed many other young girls for the job who were more qualified than I had been, but none of them were willing to go to the basement. They did have valid reasons not to.

The basement had no windows in the rooms. The basement was known to be the place where all the best students, the disciplined studiers, and the rule followers lived. Not too much excitement down in the basement. That was the reason why it was so difficult for the director to find a resident assistant to work there. No one else was willing to go there except me, and I got the job.

So I moved to the basement, and I led that group of girls LIKE A BOSS.☺ Some of my fondest college memories were made with the girls of "the basement." I helped them to liven up and enjoy college life, and they helped me to become more disciplined in my studies and class work. The once dark, bleak, dreary, lifeless basement soon became THE PLACE to live because of all the fun we were having! Good, wholesome fun mind you…we were in bible college! ☺

I've always tried to have the attitude and heart that I would be willing to do or go where no one else wanted to go. That heart attitude has served me well over my life and God has blessed it. The attitude of humility has opened doors of opportunity for me that I wouldn't have dreamed could have come my way. They have been laid before me simply because I have been willing to say "yes" in times when many others were saying "no."

My parents did set an example of great work ethic for me. They instilled in me to work hard no matter what the job was, to be true to my word, to be full of integrity and humility, to show up on time and respect the time of others, to leave things better than I found them, and to work in another man's field as if it were my own. Whether it be in a secular job or a job in ministry, a heart of humility will shine above all the others. God will honor and bless it just like he did for Ruth.

As the days passed, Ruth continued to work hard and never once took advantage of Boaz's kindness and generosity to her. When Ruth went back to Naomi, taking with her all of the provisions, Naomi inquired as to what field she had been working in. When she heard it was Boaz's field, Naomi remembered that Boaz was a relative of hers and described him as their *"kinsman redeemer"* (v. 20). Remember in chapter 1, Naomi had renamed and proclaimed herself as a now "bitter" woman, but now something leapt within the heart of Naomi as she realized who Boaz was and who he could be to the both of them.

Can you imagine the sight of poor Naomi? An old widowed woman, stooped, aged, and wrinkled, carrying the hopelessness of being a widow? What hope must have sprung up within her heart as Ruth told her about the kindness and generosity of Boaz? Though Ruth didn't realize the significance of a kinsman redeemer, Naomi certainly did. It's amazing what a little hope can do! Hope can restore joy back into a bitter woman's heart. Hope can make an old woman dream dreams again. Hope can put a pep into the tired, achy step of an old woman whose dreams for a better life were all but gone. It's no wonder the Bible tells us that *"hope is the anchor of our souls"* (Hebrews 6:19). When the seas rage and storms blow, when our souls are all but lost, the hope we have in our Heavenly Father and His promises for us can anchor, settle, and redeem our souls back to life. That's exactly what happened to Naomi. LIFE and HOPE were breathed back into her dry, parched, hopeless soul. All because of a kinsman redeemer named Boaz.

Humility attracts the attention of God's eyes and people's eyes to you.

Humility brings hope to those whose hope has been all but lost.

Humility brings God-opportunities that no man can offer.

Humility will attract a kinsman redeemer to your life.

**For Ruth, her kinsman redeemer was Boaz.
For us, it is Jesus. All because of a heart of humility and
recognition of the need to be redeemed.**

Ruth needed redemption, and so do we.

Redemption will come to us, just like it did for Ruth, through a humble heart, recognizing our need for a kinsman redeemer.

# CHAPTER 15
## *discussion questions*

1. Is humility a characteristic that people would use to describe you? Why or why not? If not, how can you change that?

2. Has there been a time in your life that your heart of humility has allowed God to open doors of opportunity for you? Explain.

3. Has there been a time when your pride has closed opportunities for you? Explain. How would you respond differently next time?

4. Describe a season in which you lost hope.

5. Has your hope been restored? If not, what will it take for that hope to be restored in your heart?

# A Kinsman Redeemer

*Ruth 2:20*

*"Naomi said to her daughter-in-law, "That man is our close relative; he is one of our kinsman-redeemers. "*

$H$*ave* you ever had someone do something for you that was completely unexpected and totally undeserved? I can't count the times my family and I have been eating at a restaurant, and when the time came for the check to be paid, our server would say, "Your meal has been taken care of." Each time we look around and watch as someone we know, or many times, whom we don't know personally, kindly and generously pays our bill. What a blessing it is each time that happens! Totally unexpected, but so graciously appreciated. Our bill had been redeemed by another. It cost us nothing.

Redemption. A word we hear regularly in the Christian world, but a word we often times, don't truly understand.

A kinsman redeemer was "a relative who could redeem," and Naomi knew exactly what that could entail for both her and Ruth. Biblical law stated that the dead husband's brother could marry the widow, and if there were no brothers, then the next of kin had the option of marrying her (Deuteronomy 25:5-10). Naomi was well past the age of child-bearing, so her excitement about a kinsman redeemer wasn't for herself but for her precious daughter-in-law, Ruth.

Ruth had spent years loving, protecting, providing, honoring, and staying close to Naomi. Now was Naomi's time to begin to give back to Ruth. By placing Ruth in a position to be redeemed, she ultimately ensured redemption for herself.

Three things were necessary for a man to be a kinsman redeemer:

1) He had to be a close relative.

2) He had to have the power to redeem, meaning he had the financial means to take care of his "redeemed".

3) He had to be willing to redeem by paying the price to buy back that which had been lost (In Ruth's case, a family and a secure future had been lost).

The word redeem means *"to buy back; to release by paying a ransom price. To make up for; to offset a fault or shortcoming."* Webster's definition of redeem is: *"to deliver from sin and its consequences by means of a sacrifice offered for the sinner."*

Redeeming someone was not a one-time act. It required the continued relationship between the redeemer and the one being redeemed. In Israel, a kinsman redeemer was one who, *by his choice, became responsible for the life of a person he redeemed as long as that person lived!*

Do you see where I'm going here? Do the above definitions and explanations of a kinsman redeemer sound like anyone you may know?

**The story of Boaz becoming a kinsman redeemer is a type and shadow of JESUS...the ultimate, perfect Redeemer.**

Boaz is a beautiful example of the picture of redemption and how Jesus came to this earth to redeem you and me. You've heard the expression: the Old Testament is Jesus concealed (everything in Old Testament pointing to Jesus), while the New Testament is Jesus revealed! Yes, Jesus humbled Himself to become a man, but that wasn't enough. There had to be a willingness to pay the awful price for our redemption by death on a cross.

Hebrews 12:2 tells us, *"but for the joy set before him"* Jesus endured the cross. Willingly and knowingly, Jesus laid down His life to become our redeemer! WE were the joy set before Him! There is absolutely nothing we can do to earn our redemption. Ruth couldn't earn her redemption either. It's simply by the love that God had for us that He sent "His only begotten Son" to die for our sins, so we wouldn't have to die for them. THAT'S amazing grace!

I once heard a ninety-eight year old woman, a minister of the Gospel, describe grace as "a response of love that is not required by law." By law, Boaz needed to redeem, but by grace he acted that redemption out in love. By law, we should pay the ultimate price for our sins... death. But by grace, God sent His Son to die for us so we wouldn't have to. The grace Boaz showed Ruth was amazing, and so is the grace shown to each one of us, every single day of our lives. It's simply AMAZING GRACE!

Boaz stooped from his position of wealth and acclaim, to help and redeem one who was not worthy. Likewise, Jesus left heaven to help and redeem you and I who are absolutely not worthy either!

The danger of walking with God for a long time is that we sometimes forget the beauty of Jesus redeeming us. May we never forget the price that was paid for our sins. May we never forget that we were once a foreigner like Ruth, not yet adopted into the family of God and in desperate need of a kinsman redeemer. May we never forget that we were once gleaning in fields not our own until one day, the eyes of God took notice of us. He saw us in our sinful, fallen states and chose to send His Son to buy us back. He made up for our shortcomings by making the ultimate sacrifice offered up to us as sinners.

May I never forget that, as a Ruth, I left home and became a foreigner in a foreign land. May I never forget the grace that was extended to me through other's kindness and generosity. May I never forget the people who saw something in me that I never saw in myself. May I never forget a God who saw my laboring in other's fields and took notice of me. May I never forget my Redeemer who bought me back, paying the ultimate price, giving up His life so that I could live mine. May I never forget to honor the One who redeemed me by serving Him all the days of my life. May I never, ever forget.

In churches all across the world, we sing songs of our Redeemer. But do we really understand that of which we sing? Do we truly recognize the desperation of what our lives would have been like without our Kinsman Redeemer? Do we fully understand the price that was paid for us? Do we have the full revelation of Jesus that, by His own choice, became responsible for our lives as we received Him as Savior and Redeemer? This was not just as a one-time act of redemption, but redemption FOR THE REST OF OUR LIVES!

Once we feel the true weight of those revelations, we begin to live our lives in a way worthy of our Redeemer. As the old hymn goes, we all owe a debt we could never repay. Our Kinsman Redeemer continues to shield and protect us under His wings. He continues to provide for us in ways that we never deserve. He lovingly speaks His promises over our lives and believes those promises for us, even when we do not.

What a great God! What a great Savior! What a great Redeemer!

# CHAPTER 16
## discussion questions

1.  Have you ever had someone do something for you that was completely unexpected and totally undeserved? If so, how did that make you feel?

2.  What would be your personal description of the word redemption?

3.  How have you seen redemption played out in your life? Either through God or by other people?

4.  Have you recognized Jesus as your personal REDEEMER, just as Boaz was Ruth's redeemer? Describe what your journey has looked like.

# chapter seventeen

# The Garment that Covers Us

*Ruth 3:1-9*

*One day Ruth's mother-in-law Naomi said to her, "My daughter, I must find a home for you, where you will be well provided for. Now Boaz, with whose women you have worked, is a relative of ours. Tonight he will be winnowing barley on the threshing floor. Wash, put on perfume, and get dressed in your best clothes. Then go down to the threshing floor, but don't let him know you are there until he has finished eating and drinking. When he lies down, note the place where he is lying. Then go and uncover his feet and lie down. He will tell you what to do."*
*"I will do whatever you say," Ruth answered. So she went down to the threshing floor and did everything her mother-in-law told her to do. When Boaz had finished eating and drinking and was in good spirits, he went over to lie down at the far end of the grain pile. Ruth approached quietly, uncovered his feet and lay down. In the middle of the night something startled the man; he turned—and*

*there was a woman lying at his feet! "Who are you?" he asked. "I am your servant Ruth," she said. "Spread the corner of your garment over me, since you are a kinsman-redeemer of our family."*

𝒜𝓈 we continue our journey into chapter 3, the instructions that we see Naomi give to Ruth may seem odd or even sexually suggestive if we don't know the context or the customs of that day. Allow me to give you an explanation as to what Naomi was asking of Ruth:

The harvesting time was over, and now it was time for the reapers to preserve the grain that had been gathered. The threshing floor was the place where the grain was separated from the harvested wheat. The wheat stalks were crushed (either by beating with sticks, or by oxen trampling them), and the valuable grain (the inner shells) were separated from the worthless chaff (the outside shell). The threshing floor was made of rock or soil and located outside the village, usually on an elevated site where the winds could blow away the lighter chaff when the crushed wheat was thrown into the air (winnowed). (Life Application Study Bible, p. 426 Ruth 3)

Naomi knew that Boaz could be found there because the owners and reapers of the fields spent the night at the threshing floor to (1) prevent anyone from stealing their harvest, and (2) to wait for their turn to thresh the grain. (Threshing was done at night because the daylight hours were spent harvesting any remaining grain.)

Stay with me here... ☺

In biblical times, baths were not the norm. They did not have the convenience of running water, so bathing was considered an "event." They had to carry the water a good distance back to their homes, and because of the work Ruth (and people in general) did, they would be quite dirty. That's why Naomi told Ruth in verse 3 to "wash and perfume yourself and put on your best clothes." Naomi's instructions meant for Ruth to take off her widow's garments that she had worked in, and by which everyone knew her social status of widowhood, and to put on her "best clothes".

While these instructions were spoken from Naomi in a literal sense, her words also carry great spiritual significance to us as well. In Isaiah 61:1-3, the word of the Lord, spoken through the prophet Isaiah says, *"The Spirit of the Lord is on me, because the Lord has anointed me to preach the good news to the poor. He has sent me to bind up the brokenhearted, to proclaim freedom for the captives and release from darkness for the prisoners, to proclaim the year of the Lord's favor and the day of vengeance of our God, to comfort all who mourn, and provide for those who grieve in Zion, to bestow on them a crown of beauty instead of ashes, the oil of gladness instead of mourning, and a garment of praise instead of a spirit of despair (heaviness)."*

Those instructions are the same for us today. As we draw near to our Kinsman Redeemer, we are to cleanse ourselves from all unrighteousness (sin), taking off our old/sinful garments (our old lives) and put on our new clothes/garments of praise/a new life in Jesus.

In verse 4, when Naomi instructs Ruth to lay at the feet of Boaz, though her advice may seem strange to us and even a bit seductive, this was not a sexual advance of any kind. Naomi was simply telling Ruth to act in accordance with Israelite custom and law. Remember, Ruth was a foreigner and did not know the customs of Israel. It was common for a servant to lie at the feet of their master and even share part of his covering. By observing this custom, Ruth would inform Boaz that he could be her kinsman redeemer, if he so chose. For the one desiring to be redeemed, it was simply an accepted practice to lie at the feet of a redeemer in this manner.

Ruth responded to Naomi's instructions in verse 5 by saying, *"I will do whatever you say."* Once again, we see the heart of obedience and humility that Ruth possessed. I cannot imagine hearing those instructions from Naomi, not knowing the Israelite customs and laws, and without question or doubt, doing exactly as Naomi said.

The question for us is this: Do we carry that same heart of obedience that we see over and over again in Ruth? Are we willing to do what God is asking of us, even if we don't understand it and without hesitation? Ruth would not have been redeemed by Boaz had she not followed Naomi's instruction to the tee. Are there Godly people in your life that can give you direction and instruction? Are there people whose hearts you can trust? Who are concerned for you? Can you follow their instructions and guidance for you, even in times when you may not see it or understand it yourself?

Verse 6 paints a beautiful picture of the character and heart of Ruth: *"So she went to the threshing floor and did everything her mother-in-law told her to do."* No questions, no hesitation, no doubt, no fear. Just complete and total obedience.

I cannot imagine what must have been going on in Ruth's mind at this time. I'm sure all the questions, doubts, and fears were there, but she didn't act on them. She acted out of pure obedience. She was vulnerable, very vulnerable. She risked rejection and humiliation, but Ruth pushed past all of those emotions and feelings and purely, wholeheartedly obeyed. God will always bless our obedience. We may not see it immediately, but with obedience comes God's blessings. God was about to honor Ruth's obedience IN A BIG WAY.

What is it that God may be asking of you? Does it seem outlandish? Uncertain? Even scary? Just obey. Carry a pure heart of humility and obedience and trust that on the other side of your obedience God's greatest blessings await you.

In verse 9, Boaz asks, *"Who are you?"* as he finds someone lying at his feet. Notice, he didn't ask what she was doing. He knew what laying at his feet meant. He asked who she was. Ruth replied to him, *"spread the corner of your garment over me, since you are my kinsman redeemer."* In Biblical culture, to spread a skirt or covering over someone was a symbolic act to offer that person protection and covering. The symbolism of this act was huge.

In Ezekiel 16:8, God is speaking and tells us this: *"as I passed by you…*

*and when I looked at you...I spread the corner of my garment over you and covered your nakedness. I gave you my solemn oath and entered into a covenant with you, declares the Sovereign Lord, and YOU BECAME MINE."* In the same manner that Boaz would redeem Ruth, God redeems us!

**The precious picture of Boaz covering and redeeming Ruth is a prophetic act of how one day God would send His Son to cover our sins and bring redemption to His people.**

When Ruth asked Boaz to cover her, she was humbly and vulnerably declaring: "I NEED A REDEEMER. I AM A WIDOW, DISGRACED, WITH NO INHERITANCE OR HOPE FOR A SECURE FUTURE. YOU CAN TAKE MY SHAME, MY POVERTY, THE BLEAKNESS OF MY FUTURE, AND GIVE ME AN INHERITANCE. YOU CAN TOTALLY AND COMPLETELY REDEEM ME, IF YOU WILL."

In acknowledging the helplessness of her condition, Ruth is a picture of the helpless state of every person needing a redeemer. Ruth ran a HUGE risk of rejection as she lay at Boaz's feet. She was completely and utterly at the mercy of her kinsman redeemer. All her life, her hopes, her dreams, her security, her provision, and her future was dependent upon the decision of Boaz. I pray, as you read these words, you picture in your mind the helpless state of this precious girl laying at Boaz's feet. I pray that you feel what she may have been feeling. I pray you sense her desperation within your own heart. Ruth had lived a hard, difficult life. She knew what great loss felt like. She knew what it felt like to walk through "the valley of the shadow of death." She knew what it felt like to leave family and homeland to follow

God's purposes and plans for her life. She knew the weight of being single and having to provide for herself and Naomi.

Why do I want you to put yourself in Ruth's shoes? Because without Jesus, that is the same exact condition we find ourselves. Through the mercy, grace, and love of God, we can run to the feet of Jesus and humbly ask the same question that Ruth asked, "Lord, will you spread your covering and your forgiveness over me and redeem me? Will you take my shame, my disgrace, my brokenness, my pain, and my regret, and will you redeem me? Will you buy me back and bring me into Your family? Will you give me a hope for my future? Can you forgive me of all the sins I've committed against you? Can you give me a new name? A new purpose? A new future and eternal inheritance?"

Just as Boaz accepted the humble request of a foreign girl named Ruth, so does our Heavenly Father accept our humble request of needing a Redeemer and a Savior. If you haven't yet fallen at His feet and asked for His redemption and covering of sins over your life, will you do so now? Like Ruth, will you humbly ask for His forgiveness? Will you acknowledge today your need for a Savior? If so, I would love for you to pray this prayer with me:

# dear Heavenly Father

I am in desperate need of a Redeemer and a Savior. Like Ruth, I've walked through some dark valleys and difficult times. At times, I've felt like a foreigner in a strange land. I humbly fall at your feet and ask of You to take my sin, my shame, my hurts, my pains, my disappointments, my doubts, and my fears, and cover them and redeem them.

I thank you that before I ever recognized that I needed a Savior, you sent your Son Jesus to die for my sins, so that I wouldn't have to. I receive your forgiveness and your redemption today. I commit to serve You all the days of my life. Jesus, You are now, not only my Redeemer and Savior, but you are also Lord over my life today.

## in Jesus name. Amen

If you prayed that prayer, welcome to the family of God. Call someone and let them know that you prayed the prayer of salvation. If you are not already plugged into a healthy, life-giving church, find one and begin your journey with God and His people.

There are great days ahead for you. They won't all be easy, but your Redeemer is with you and is covering you. He has a great future in store for you!

# CHAPTER 17
## discussion questions

**1.** If you were in Ruth's shoes, what would your reaction have been to Naomi had she given you those same instructions?

**2.** Describe a specific time in your life when obedience to God was difficult.

**3.** In the end, did you end up obeying Him? If not, why? If you had to do it all over again, would you obey?

**4.** Share how God's blessings have followed your obedience.

**5.** Would you be described as a woman of obedience? If so, how?

**6.** What is God asking of you now that will require some BIG steps of obedience? What will be required of you to take that step?

**7.** In what areas of your life have you experienced or are asking for the covering of your Redeemer?

**8.** Did you pray the prayer of salvation at the end of this chapter? If so, please let your small group leader or a trusted Godly friend know. It's so important that you connect to Godly relationships. If not, would you consider praying that prayer now?

*chapter eighteen*

# To All the Single Girls

*Ruth 3:10-12*

*"The Lord bless you, my daughter," he replied. "This kindness is greater than that which you showed earlier: You have not run after the younger men, whether rich or poor. And now, my daughter, don't be afraid. I will do for you all you ask. All the people of my town know that you are a woman of noble character. Although it is true that I am a kinsman-redeemer of our family, there is another who is more closely related than I."*

$I\!n$ these verses, Boaz accepts Ruth's request to be her kinsman redeemer. He also states two clear observations of Ruth that are totally applicable to us today, especially you single girls. ☺

Boaz noticed that Ruth "did not run after the younger men, whether rich or poor". All of the towns people of Bethlehem had also noticed that Ruth *"was a woman of noble character,"* or as some versions describe, "a virtuous woman." It's the same word (virtuous) that is used to describe the Godly woman, wife, and mother of Proverbs 31. (That's another book for another day!) Wow! I wonder if those same observations can be said of us, especially our single girls?

The word virtuous or virtue means *"conforming one's life and conduct to moral and ethical principles; moral excellence; right conduct; a distinction between right and wrong."* Conforming indicates that it's a choice we must make, a lifestyle we must choose because we're not naturally born virtuous. Forgive me for sounding a bit old-fashioned, but moral and ethical principles in this day and age are all but a forgotten way of life. The culture of our world today tells us "if it feels good, do it", "there is no right or wrong", etc. Because of that mindset, our nation, our communities, and our families are paying the high price of no moral or ethical standards today.

**A woman of virtue is one who is led by her principles,**
**her morals, her convictions, and her standards.**
**It is not old-fashioned. It is Biblical.**

It's still as true today as it was in Ruth's day. Though customs and cultures may have changed, Godly, biblical morals and principles have not. A woman of godly character and principles will stand out today, just as Ruth stood out to her newly found community and people.

Single women: you do not have to "run after the young men", no matter what our culture screams at you. The same hand of God that led Ruth divinely to the field of Boaz will be the same Hand that will lead and guide you divinely to your Boaz, or your Boaz to you.

Mothers of daughters: Godly, principled, virtuous mothers will raise Godly, principled, virtuous daughters. Your daughters are watching you. Not by the words that you speak necessarily, but by the life you live before them. Your daughters don't need another best friend. They have plenty of friends. Your daughters need a mother. No one else on planet earth can be a mother to your daughter except you.

The Hebrew word for virtuous is "chayil" which means "strength, ability, might, and power." That's a strong woman, not a weak, pitiful one. A virtuous woman is one who reaches down within herself and finds the strength, ability, might, and power she needs to overcome whatever she must walk through. Whatever the trial, the test, or the circumstance before you, you are ABLE and YOU CAN DO IT. Ruth's life exemplifies that beautifully.

I see women everyday who don't think they can do "it", whatever "it" may be at that particular time in their life. They don't think they have the strength, ability, might, or power; they don't think they possess that kind of inner strength. If Jesus has become your Redeemer and Savior, the Bible tells us that *"the same spirit that raised Jesus from the dead"* now lives in you and I! (Romans 8:11) That's a lot of STRENGTH, ABILITY, MIGHT, AND POWER living in us!

At eighteen years of age, when I went to bible college, I was a bit of an exception. I did not go to bible college to find a husband. I went to bible college to pursue the calling of God that He had placed on my life. I never once remember thinking to myself, "I've got to find a husband." Up until that point, I had never even gone on a date. NOT ONE. During my high school years, I never had a boyfriend and didn't go to any of my school's dances or parties. I didn't attend my Senior Prom, and I did this for one reason: I knew what those environments were like. They were a place to party and drink alcohol and hookup with whatever guy that came along that night. So I didn't go at all. Why? Simply because I loved God and I wanted to please Him in all that I did. Honestly, that was my heart over thirty years ago, and it's still my heart today - To love and honor God in all that I say and do. I'm certainly not perfect, and at times, I fail miserably just as many of you do. But the question of my heart back then, as well as today, in my decision making is this "God, would you be proud and honored in this decision?" Would I feel the smile of God upon this decision? If I feel that it is a yes, then I go forward full of faith. If there is a hesitancy in my heart, or I hear a clear "no", then I walk away from the opportunity or say "no" to that person. To me, it really is that simple.

As a young, bible college student, I had better things to do than to "run after young men" in trying to find a husband. As I stayed faithful to God and to getting an education that would prepare me for a lifetime of ministry, the Divine Hand of God that led me to a specific bible college many hours away from my hometown was the same Hand of God that led my future husband many hours away from his hometown to the particular bible college where I "just so happened" to be. Girls, do not for a moment believe the lie of the enemy when he tells you that God cannot or will not move heaven and earth to allow the paths of you and your future husband to cross and intersect. He will and He can just like He did for me, and just as He did for Ruth. If you are determined to love God and follow Him on the road He's laid out for you, you must trust that He has your future husband on a similar road, and when it's His time, your paths will intersect.

Do you trust God with every area of your life, even with whom you are to marry? Do you trust Him when the future seems uncertain? Do you trust Him when you are lonely and so deeply desire to be married and have a family of your own? This is what I have found to be true over all of these years: God is so trustworthy. He is worthy of our trust. ALL of it. Just as God saw a young, Moabite girl leaving her home land in hopes of a better life, just as His eyes saw the desires of her heart for a better future, just as He recognized Ruth's need for a Redeemer, He sees exactly where you are too. He sees the desires of your heart. He sees the fields where you are laboring. He sees your heart cry for a promise yet to be fulfilled. YOU CAN TRUST HIM. Even when it seems that God is nowhere to be found, He's actually closer to you than you could ever imagine. He is IN YOUR FIELD, and He is preparing a great future and a great Boaz, just for you!

# CHAPTER 18
## discussion questions

**1.** If you are currently married, share with your small group what your life looked like as a single girl. The good, the bad, and the ugly!☺

**2.** If you are single, share with your group how you are currently navigating your season of singleness.

**3.** What are some of the benefits of being single in today's world? What are some of the challenges?

**4.** If you are a mother or grandmother of single daughters or grand-daughters, how has this chapter better equipped you to help them walk through this season of their lives?

**5.** If you are single, how has this chapter helped with your perspective in your season of singleness? What changes do you need to make to have a better perspective?

# Why Is it so Hard to Sit Still?

*Ruth 3:2-18*

*Although it is true that I am a kinsman-redeemer of our family, there is another who is more closely related than I. Stay here for the night, and in the morning if he wants to do his duty as your kinsman-redeemer, good; let him redeem you. But if he is not willing, as surely as the Lord lives I will do it. Lie here until morning." So she lay at his feet until morning, but got up before anyone could be recognized; and he said, "No one must know that a woman came to the threshing floor." He also said, "Bring me the shawl you are wearing and hold it out." When she did so, he poured into it six measures of barley and placed the bundle on her. Then he went back to town. When Ruth came to her mother-in-law, Naomi asked, "How did it go, my daughter?" Then she told her everything Boaz had done for her and added, "He gave me these six measures of barley, saying, 'Don't go back to your mother-in-law empty-handed.' "Then Naomi said, "Wait, my daughter,*

*until you find out what happens. For the man will not rest*
*until the matter is settled today."*


$\mathcal{A}$y we close out chapter 3 of Ruth, we see Boaz's offer to redeem Ruth. However, Boaz had heard that there was possibly another relative, who was closer kin than he was. The law stated that Boaz must first check with the closer relative to give him the opportunity to redeem Ruth himself or give Boaz permission to redeem her. So the following morning, Ruth went back to Naomi and explained all that had transpired over the night. Naomi's response to Ruth's explanation was, surprisingly, *"Wait my daughter, until you find out what will happen."* (v18) The NKJV says it this way, *"Sit still my daughter until you know how the matter will fall."* In other words, Naomi was saying "Ruth, now we wait. We are not going to make something happen. You have done everything that you can do. Now, we will trust God, and we will trust Boaz to be true to his word." What great wisdom from a woman who, only two chapters before, was praying death down on herself and describing herself as bitter!

The evening before, Naomi had told Ruth in great detail all she was to do. Ruth had obeyed to the letter, but now, Naomi was telling her to wait and to sit still.

Do you remember how difficult it was to sit still when you were a young child? Time seemed to come to a complete standstill whenever those dreaded words were spoken. "Just sit still." Everything within you wanted to get up, stand up, or jump up and run around just knowing that you couldn't. Whether it was in a doctor's office, at a church service, on a long car ride, or simply because you were being punished, those three words made the realization of you having lost the freedom of running about all the more painful.

As a young child, "just sit still" were the most dreadful words you could hear. But as a grown adult, I've come to realize that those same words aren't any easier to hear or to obey. In fact, I think they are harder to hear now than they were when I was a child.

If you've ever had to sit still for an extended period of time, you know how physically painful it can be. I've been on ten+ hour flights to England, and I've been on twenty-six+ hour flights to Africa, and only one word can describe sitting still for that long...EXCRUCIATING!

It is truly agonizing to sit still when there is absolutely nothing else to do. One can only read so many magazines, watch so many movies, or sleep for so long, before you are literally going stir crazy in your mind! My legs ached and throbbed, my back and head pounded as my feet swelled up with each passing moment. Am I sounding dramatic yet?☺ I think you get the picture, especially if you've been on one of those extended flights. EXCRUCIATING!

Just when you think that the words "sit still" could not be more difficult to hear, one day you hear those same words from your Heavenly Father, whispering to your heart "just sit still". Have you ever been in one of those seasons? After doing all you know to do, you still don't see any results of your prayers, petitions, or requests to God, then you find Him asking you to sit still and wait. Painful, isn't it? Maybe even excruciating?

Several years ago, I was working on this very book. (Yes, it took me TEN YEARS to finally complete it, but more on that later.) I knew that God had asked me to write this. No question about it. I had been diligent about this project, spending long hours and days pouring my heart out on paper. One day, as I walked through my kitchen, I asked God, "Is there anything else I should be doing with this? Marketing? Promoting? Finding a publisher? What is the next step once I finish this? What's the next phone call I should make? The next appointment I need to set once I complete this book?" I clearly heard the voice of God speak to my heart, answering my question by saying, "Sit still my daughter, until you see how the matter will fall."

I immediately recognized the verse from Ruth 3:18. Certainly not the words I wanted or even expected to hear. Ironically, as I was in the process of writing a book about Ruth, God instructed me the same way Naomi instructed Ruth, "just sit still". I found myself having to obey just as Ruth had to obey. Several years ago, when I heard His instruction to me, I was feeling that this book project was coming to an end. I felt as if the season were about to change, that I was about to get a phone call or a proposal for my book, the book God had asked me to write. Instead of getting any of those things, I got a "sit still my daughter". I found myself, again, having to relinquish control of what I thought should happen and the timing in which it should happen. I had to give up control.

**I realize now that when I am obedient to sitting still,
I allow the hand of God to work on my behalf
in ways that I don't even know.**

I have lived long enough and have made enough mistakes in not waiting to know that if I have my hand in something, trying to make it happen, then I am ultimately tying God's hands from working for me. I would much rather God's hands work for me instead of my own!

Just like Ruth, I am a girl with initiative and determination. No one has to tell me twice to do something. I'm a "pray, then get up and do something about it" girl. Often times that spirit and heart have served me well. In other times, God tells me to sit still and wait. It about kills me, but I obey because I love Him, and I trust Him with my life.

I've learned from experience that sitting still never gets easier, but it's WELL WORTH THE WAIT. As I look back to that time in my kitchen when I heard God's voice speak to me, I now know that it just wasn't the time for the completion of this book to happen. God wasn't finished completing ME. There was still much work for Him to do in my heart concerning my family and the pain that was still there. All these years later, I know it's time. There's been a new level of healing and wholeness that God has brought to my broken heart, and it wouldn't have happened unless I obeyed His instruction to "sit still, my daughter". Maybe there's a wrestle on the inside of your heart, wondering if there is anything else you can do? You may be wondering, "Are there any more prayers that I can pray? Any more conversations I need to have? Is there something else I should be doing?" Just maybe God wants to speak those same words to you, too: "Sit still my daughter, until you see how the matter will fall." Rest and wait with peace, knowing that God is working on your behalf, even if you don't see it or understand it.

I assure you, it won't be easy, but it will be worth the wait.

# CHAPTER 19

## discussion questions

**1.** How did you feel, as a young child, when you were told to "be still"?

**2.** As an adult, what is your first reaction when you hear that same request from God?

**3.** Describe a season in your life when there was nothing else for you to do but to "be still". How did you handle that season? What was the outcome of your "sitting still"?

**4.** Has there been a time when you did not sit still and took matters into your own hands? Explain how that played out and some of the consequences you might have suffered for not sitting still.

**5.** Why is it so hard to relinquish control over a particular situation? Does relinquishing control come easy for you, or is it difficult for you? Explain why or why not.

**6.** What current situation is God asking of you to "sit still, my daughter, until you see how the matter will fall."?

**7.** Take a moment in prayer to relinquish total control of that situation over to God.

# The Benefits of Waiting

*Ruth 3:18*
*Then Naomi said, "Wait, my daughter, until you find out*
*what happens. For the man will not rest until the matter*
*is settled today."*

*a* clear sign of how mature we are is how patient we are in waiting. The younger the child, the harder it is to wait. A sure sign of our Christian maturity is how we handle a season of waiting.

How do we know if God is asking us to wait when nothing else is happening? It's in those seasons of waiting that we must trust what God has promised us He will do it, but it will be in His time, not ours. The yes's and even the no's are easy to hear, at least we have a clear answer. It is the answer of "wait" or "sit still" that can be so difficult not only for us to hear, but also to obey.

One of my biggest mistakes in ministry and a clear sign of my immaturity in those early years was when I would hear God clearly speak to my heart, but I expected the answer to come right away. When the answer didn't come immediately, I became discouraged thinking I had not heard from God in the first place. As I look back to my younger self, I can now see how immature and misguided that thinking was. There are some divine, prophetic things that God has spoken to me over the years, and some of those things, more than twenty-seven years later, have still not come to pass. It doesn't change the fact that God spoke them to me. I must continue to wait patiently for His promises.

I have learned this truth over all these years though: God will speak His promises to us. Then, we enter into a season of waiting because it is in the time of waiting that God prepares our hearts to be ready to receive His answer and His promise. **Once God sees that our hearts and our character can withstand His promises, then He sends us the answer.**

In Genesis, God spoke His promise to Abraham. Abraham then had to wait twenty-five years for the promise of a son to come to pass. When the answer did come in the form of his son, Isaac, God asked the unthinkable...to sacrifice the very promise that Abraham had so patiently waited and believed for. As Isaac was laid on the altar and God saw the obedient heart of Abraham, He provided another sacrifice. Eventually, Abraham saw the promise of God fulfilled as he became the father of the Jewish nation.

The promise was spoken. The season of waiting (and even testing) came. Then, God's promises were fulfilled in Abraham and his descendants (Genesis 22:15-18, Hebrews 6:13-15).

Psalm 46:10 tells us to "be still and know that I am God." Was the Psalmist suggesting that the only way we can truly know God, is to be still? To wait on Him?

Often times, only when we come to the end of our own resources, when there are few distractions left to us, when we've done all we know to do, does it become possible to be quiet, to wait, and to sit still. God is very patient with us when we are trying our hardest to be patient with Him.

There are great benefits during our seasons of waiting:

## 1) Our own hearts are revealed to us.

Sometimes, we never see our own hearts clearly, until we sit still. God already knows what is within our hearts. He just wants us to see for ourselves. These seasons allow God to prune away the things in our hearts that do not need to be there - unforgiveness, offense, hurts, fears, etc. We won't know what our hearts contain unless we are still.

## 2) It brings the right perspective.

Sitting still allows us to look at the bigger picture. It gives us a thirty-thousand feet view into our circumstances that we might not have seen had we not been asked to sit still or to wait.

## 3) Helps us to realize that we were never in control in the first place.

There is nothing like a season of waiting and sitting still for us to realize that God is God, and we are not. No matter how hard we try, we cannot control a season of waiting. We cannot throw a fit to cause God's hand to move quicker. We simply cannot do it. Moments of sitting still will make us relinquish our control over to God's control.

## 4) It helps build our trust in God.

Real trust is built in the waiting and in the sitting still. Either we trust Him or we don't. It's never more clear than when we have to wait.

## 5) It brings about the peace of God.

It's amazing! Once we relinquish control over to God and admit to ourselves and to Him that we never really had the control, peace can flood through our hearts and minds.

As long as we're wrestling in our hearts to make something happen, peace will not be evident. Once the wrestling stops, peace can then come.

## 6) It puts us in the correct position.

We become desperate for God again. We recognize how much we

need Him. We become His children again, and God remains our Father. Our wise, patient, loving, gracious Father that He's always been. It sometimes takes a season of sitting still for us to remember that.

## 7 ) We are able to hear God's voice more clearly.

Sitting still takes away all of the distractions that can drown out the voice of God in our hearts. We stop listening to our own voices and the negative voices of others and wait to hear His voice. It is in our times of waiting that His precious, affirming words can be heard so much more clearly.

## 8 ) Christ's character can be formed in us.

Seasons of waiting allow God to more perfectly form His character within us. This is so necessary as He is preparing our hearts to receive His answers and His promises. His love, His mercy, His grace, and His forgiveness are more readily received by our hearts as we wait on Him.

Sweet girl, please do not despise your season of waiting or sitting still. There is great purpose in the waiting. The promise will be worth the wait. Just "sit still, my daughter, until you see how the matter will fall."

God is in control of that very situation that you have made yourself crazy about. He is working while you are waiting. He can handle the pressure and the weight of what you may be walking through. The weight is about to crush you, but He can easily carry it.

Give it over to Him now. Relinquish your control over to His control. Trust Him with that precious promise completely. Allow Him to form His character in you perfectly. Receive the love and grace He desires to pour out on you wholeheartedly and with a grateful heart.

Your answer is coming.

Your promise is on its way.

Just sit, be still, and wait.

# CHAPTER 20

## discussion questions

As a small group, or in your personal time of journaling, read over the benefits of waiting that I discussed in this chapter. Take some time with each point. Ask yourself (or your small group) the following questions:

1. Have I experienced this truth personally? If so, how?

2. Of the eight benefits, which ones come easier for me?

3. Which ones are the most difficult to implement in my life? Why is that?

4. What is the one main point/benefit that God is placing His finger on in my life to improve upon?

5. What specifically will that improvement look like?

6. Are you willing to make the necessary adjustments so that your heart can remain in a posture of "stillness" as you wait on God to bring about your answer or promise?

# The Restoration of a Family

*Ruth 4:1-15*

*"Meanwhile Boaz went up to the town gate and sat down there just as the kinsman-redeemer he had mentioned came along. Boaz said, "Come over here, my friend, and sit down." So he went over and sat down.*

*Boaz took ten of the elders of the town and said, "Sit here," and they did so. Then he said to the kinsman-redeemer, "Naomi, who has come back from Moab, is selling the piece of land that belonged to our relative Elimelech. I thought I should bring the matter to your attention and suggest that you buy it in the presence of these seated here and in the presence of the elders of my people. If you will redeem it, do so. But if you will not, tell me, so I will know. For no one has the right to do it except you, and I am next in line." "I will redeem it," he said. Then Boaz said, "On the day you buy the land from Naomi, you also acquire Ruth the Moabite, the dead man's widow, in order to maintain the name of the dead with his property."*

At this, the kinsman-redeemer said, "Then I cannot redeem it because I might endanger my own estate. You redeem it yourself. I cannot do it." (Now in earlier times in Israel, for the redemption and transfer of property to become final, one party took off his sandal and gave it to the other. This was the method of legalizing transactions in Israel.) So the kinsman-redeemer said to Boaz, "Buy it yourself." And he removed his sandal. Then Boaz announced to the elders and all the people, "Today you are witnesses that I have bought from Naomi all the property of Elimelech, Kilion and Mahlon. I have also acquired Ruth the Moabite, Mahlon's widow, as my wife, in order to maintain the name of the dead with his property, so that his name will not disappear from among his family or from his hometown. Today you are witnesses!" Then the elders and all the people at the gate said, "We are witnesses. May the Lord make the woman who is coming into your home like Rachel and Leah, who together built up the family of Israel. May you have standing in Ephrathah and be famous in Bethlehem. Through the offspring the Lord gives you by this young woman, may your family be like that of Perez, whom Tamar bore to Judah." So Boaz took Ruth and she became his wife. When he made love to her, the Lord enabled her to conceive, and she gave birth to a son. The women said to Naomi: "Praise be to the Lord, who this day has not left you without a kinsman-redeemer. May he become famous throughout Israel! He will renew your life and sustain you in your old age.

*For your daughter-in-law, who loves you and who is better to you than seven sons, has given him birth."*

The book of Ruth began with a family, and now the book of Ruth ends with a family. The family in chapter 1 looks very different from the family we see in chapter 4. A lot of life happened between chapter 1 and chapter 4. Years passed. Heartache happened. Disappointment came. Promises seemed lost. However, eventually a lot of redemption, grace, and restoration came back to Ruth and Naomi.

Boaz did go to the closer relative and give him the opportunity of redeeming Ruth. After counting the costs to redeem Ruth, the relative chose not to. This opened the door of opportunity for Boaz to become her redeemer.

I honestly don't know if there's a more beautiful and poignant verse in all the book of Ruth, than verse 13 in chapter 4: *"So Boaz took Ruth and she became his wife."* Boaz, a wealthy, honorable, Godly man of great standing in Bethlehem, took Ruth, who was a Moabite girl, a foreigner, widow, a destitute woman with no future, inheritance, children, or hope to become his wife. Suddenly, life changed forever for Ruth and for Naomi. Just when you thought the story could not end more beautifully, we realize that it was not just Ruth that had been redeemed, but it was also her mother-in-law Naomi. (v 9-10) It was a package deal of redemption. ☺

It doesn't matter how many times I've read those few verses in chapter 4 over the past sixteen years, those words still bring tears to my eyes. I cannot even read them aloud in a message that I am speaking without my voice cracking and tears streaming down my face. It is not just the words that move me. IT'S THE HOPE THAT THOSE WORDS REPRESENT, not just for Ruth and Naomi, but for ME, and for YOU. They move me because I have been a Ruth, and I have been a Naomi and have felt no hope for my future. I'm also moved by them because I know what redemption feels like as a Ruth and as a Naomi and as Heidi. I know what restored hope and restored purpose feel like. I know what dead dreams coming back to life feel like, and so did Ruth and Naomi. I know what grace and forgiveness feel like. I know what unconditional love feels like because I know the One who freely gives that love. I am humbled. I am grateful, and I will spend the rest of my life honoring and loving The One who, so long ago, redeemed my life as well.

As Ruth and Naomi began to prepare for a wedding only a few months earlier, they were preparing to leave Moab, without husbands, without children, without an inheritance, knowing that their futures looked very destitute and bleak as widows. Though their hearts had been severely tested, they continued to place their faith in God, and He proved His faithfulness to them in a great way!

Verse 13 tells us that Ruth *"...gave birth to a son."* Ruth had not known the joy of motherhood until now. Ruth was once a stranger to Israel and their God. She didn't know it at the time, but she was now becoming a significant part in the lineage of our Lord and Savior, Jesus

Christ! Every Jewish woman in Israel should have been more eligible for this honor, but God chose Ruth. He divinely placed her in the blessing and lineage of His own Son, Jesus.

Ruth 4:17 describes this Divine lineage: *"And they named him Obed. He was the father of Jesse, the father of David."*

Ruth and Boaz's son would become the grandfather of King David!

Sweet girl reading these words, don't you ever think for one moment that God cannot choose you and use you for His glory and eternal purposes! Regardless of your background, your past, your sins, and your mistakes; regardless of your family name, reputation, and up-bringing; regardless of what people have said you would never do or never become, when God redeems you, He also redeems your story!

**God can find you in your obscurity, gleaning in a foreign field. He can find you even if you feel that no one in the world knows who you are or what is in your heart to do for Him.**

Not only will He find you, He will redeem all that has been stolen, broken, and lost in your life! He will breathe life back into your dry, parched soul and your dead, long forgotten dreams. Not only can God do it, HE DESIRES TO DO IT even more than you want Him to!

Not only did God's blessing come to Ruth, it also poured over Naomi as well. The prayer of blessing came from the women of Bethlehem, spoken to their old, once bitter friend Naomi. They even exclaimed, *"Naomi has a son!"* (v 16-17). This son would be a promise restored not only to Ruth, but also to Naomi. God was restoring back to Naomi all that she had lost as well. In Joel 2:25, God declares such a promise: *"I will repay you for the years that the locusts (the enemy) have eaten away (or stolen)."* The prayer of blessing was spoken over Naomi also. Naomi never set out to become redeemed herself. Her desire for redemption was for Ruth, but while God (through Boaz) redeemed Ruth, His redemption included Naomi as well. All the years of heartache, pain, and loss were redeemed back to Naomi. The same woman who had named herself "Mara, the bitter one", found herself under the blessings, provisions, and restored promises of God.

**The wonder of redemption is that it restores us to a place of greater blessing than we experienced before our unfortunate losses in our lives.**

It is never too late, and you are never too old to receive God's beautiful redemption! Just as Romans 8:28 promises us, God really can *"work ALL things together for our good"*. Just look at Ruth and Naomi.

As we've read and journeyed through the lives of Naomi and Ruth, I pray you've seen your life and the lives of your family represented in them. Just as with Naomi and with Ruth, there is redemption and restoration promised for you and your family. It may take a while to see it. It may not look like what you had envisioned, but the first step is to begin your journey. The story of redemption and restoration is a beautiful one, and it can become a beautiful story in your life as well!

# CHAPTER 21
## discussion questions

1. In what specific areas are you asking God for restoration, either in your own life and family, or in extended family or friend relationships?

2. What part, if any, do you feel that God is asking you to play in that restoration? Are you willing to obey? If not, why not?

3. What part of Ruth and Boaz's love story blesses you most? Explain.

4. What hope has been restored in your heart as you've read their story?

5. What area of your life do you need to believe Romans 8:28 for?

6. Make a decision today to begin looking for the GOOD that God is doing in your life and the lives of your family members or friends.

# The Dysfunctional Family Tree

*Ruth 4:16-22*

*Then Naomi took the child in her arms and cared for him.*
*The women living there said, "Naomi has a son!" And*
*they named him Obed. He was the father of Jesse, the fa-*
*ther of David. This, then, is the family line of Perez: Pe-*
*rez was the father of Hezron, Hezron the father of Ram,*
*Ram the father of Amminadab, Amminadab the father of*
*Nahshon, Nahshon the father of Salmon, Salmon the fa-*
*ther of Boaz, Boaz the father of Obed, Obed the father of*
*Jesse, and Jesse the father of David.*

*a* few years ago, when our oldest daughter was in college, I
received a phone call from her asking me a question: "Mom, in my
archeology class, we have to draw our family tree. Can you tell me

what ours looks like?" To the rest of the world, that may seem like a very simple question with a very simple answer. But to me, it was anything but simple. As I awkwardly tried to talk through what my side of the family tree would look like, there were more questions than answers. My family tree was not as simple as drawing a pretty, healthy, normal tree and adding names to the branches. I had no idea what those branches even looked like, much less the names that belonged on them. The few branches I could recall were broken, split, and not healthy looking at all.

If you are reading this with even a remotely normal, healthy family, you have no understanding as to what I am saying, but if dysfunction is a word you have used to describe your family over and over again, then you know EXACTLY what I am talking about. Growing up, my parents didn't talk a lot about extended family members, where they came from, and what they did. In fact, we didn't talk about it at all. I knew it back then, and I certainly know it now; there were a lot of family secrets. A LOT. No one talked about any of them. Thus, the term "family secrets." That term wasn't even used. No words were used. We just didn't talk about any of it, and if we had any questions, they were disregarded or dismissed as if we had not even asked them. To this day, I still don't know "the secrets."

As I tried to explain this unusual family tree to my daughter, I finally just said: "Honestly Hillary, I just don't know. I don't know the branches and I don't know the names. So I guess my side of the family tree will just have to look like one, plain trunk with no branches, and don't even try to explain it to your professor. Just trust me on this one!" Sadly, my daughter knew exactly what I was talking about because she and her brother and sister had had front row seats to the breakdown of the relationship in my family. My daughter was very gracious of my request and acted like it was no big deal. Part of her family tree was just going be deformed looking on her paper. I do know, however, that it was a bigger deal to her than she led on. Thankfully, she loved her mother enough to hold it together so I wouldn't be more guilt-ridden and ashamed than I already was. I was so thankful for her grace and God's grace over my crazy, dysfunctional family tree.

The final verses of the book of Ruth close out with a portion of Jesus' genealogy listed. Matthew, chapter 1 gives us the entire listing of His family tree. Matthew 1:1-6, 16: *"A record of the genealogy of Jesus Christ the son of David, the son of Abraham: Abraham was the father of Isaac, Isaac the father of Jacob, Jacob the father of Judah and his brothers, Judah the father of Perez and Zerah, whose mother was* **TAMAR***, Perez the father of Hezron, Hezron the father of Ram, Ram the father of Amminadab, Amminadab the father of Nahshon, Nahshon the father of Salmon, Salmon the father of Boaz, whose mother was* **RAHAB***, Boaz the father of Obed, whose mother was* **RUTH***, Obed the father of Jesse, and Jesse the father of King David. David was the father of Solomon, whose mother had been Uriah's wife,* **BATHSHEBA***….."*

*"….and Jacob the father of Joseph, the husband of* **MARY***, of whom was born Jesus, who is called Christ."*

It does not matter how many times I speak a message on Jesus' genealogy or how many times I read it, each and every time, as I read the names of Jesus' family line of women, tears pour down my face. Why? Because of the hope that those names, those pasts, those broken families bring to me. Jesus' family tree is just as dysfunctional as mine, proving the fact that the health  or the dysfunction of your family tree isn't what God is looking at when He chooses someone to use. God looks at our hearts, not our family trees! And all God's people said, "AMEN!" ☺

Between Abraham and the birth of Jesus, there were forty-two generations of people. Hundreds of years of men and women, but only five women were mentioned by name in Jesus' family tree, and their reputations were nothing to brag about! Talk about some family secrets!

Tamar was the mother of Perez who seduced her father-in-law to get pregnant. Rahab was the mother of Boaz, but in her early life was a harlot and prostitute. Ruth, as we know, was a Moabitess, a foreigner. Bathsheba was an adulterer, but sweet Mary was a precious, innocent teenage girl, chosen by God to be the mother of Jesus.

All but Mary had very scarred, sinful, dark pasts. God divinely chose to have Jesus' family tree written in the Bible for us to clearly see. It's almost as if we can hear Jesus saying to us as we read those names, "I have been there too." To the lonely, to the discouraged, to the rejected, to the ashamed, Jesus says, "I have been there. I know what dysfunction is. I know what a broken family tree feels like."

Remember the description of a dysfunctional family? "When something is broken within the family but no one knows how to fix it."

Does that describe your family? It certainly describes mine! We've been broken for as long as I can remember without the hope of it ever being fixed. There are absolutely no PERFECT families but there are HEALTHY families. Healthy families still have brokenness, still have problems, still have disagreements and still have arguments.

**The difference between a healthy family and a dysfunctional family is that a healthy family knows how to fix themselves.**

They understand that grace, love, and forgiveness must be freely given and freely received in order for that family to remain healthy. They do not hold grudges, and they do not hold family members mistakes and shortcomings over their heads, only to use it against them time and time again. Healthy families choose to see the best in their family members, understanding that family sticks with one another through good times and bad.

Dysfunctional families are the exact opposite of ALL OF THE ABOVE. They refuse to see and acknowledge the brokenness in their family, and because of their refusal to recognize the truth of what's really happening, they forgo the hope of ever being able to fix what is broken. Dysfunctional families still love one another, but they can only love out of their own brokenness, never out of a place of wholeness.

Please allow me to speak some hope and truth to those of you who have grown up in or are currently part of a dysfunctional family. It is never too late to get help. Even if the other family members refuse help (and most of them more than likely will), you can still ask for and receive help. Healing can come to your life, even if other family members refuse it. Whether it be through a professional counselor, a pastor, or trusted, Godly leader in your life, help is available. You must, however, take the initiative to get the necessary help.

There are two valuable lessons that I've learned throughout my life concerning the brokenness in family:

## 1) God wastes nothing.

Time is not wasted. Pain is not wasted. Years are not wasted. Brokenness is not wasted. Heartache is not wasted. Tears are not wasted. GOD WASTES NOTHING. As I look back over the years, God has used ALL of what I've walked through and continue to walk through to form in my heart a greater representation of His heart. Without a doubt, I would not be the woman I am today had I not traveled down a road of hurt, rejection, heartache, and much, much pain. The promise of Romans 8:28 has proven true in my life many times over. God has truly *"...worked ALL things together for my good"*. Now, when He was working them out in me, it didn't feel good at the time. But looking back now, IT WAS GOOD. VERY GOOD.

## 2) God never leaves us lacking.

If anyone who didn't know me was around me for any length of time, they would never know all that I have walked through concerning my family. Only by the grace of God is there no "stinch" or residue from the fire that I have walked through in my life. (Daniel 3:27) No one would look at me and see a "lack" in my life. You would never know that I have not had a healthy relationship with my mother. You would never know the deep pain and brokenness that I have experienced. You wouldn't see the wound of rejection that I carried for so many years. You wouldn't see the loneliness that once ached in my heart. You wouldn't see all the tears I have cried for years and years and years.

God has more than made up for any lack that I once had in my life. How? By the divine relationships He has placed in my life. Everywhere I turn, there are women, and couples, and friends, and pastors, and godly leaders that have filled any gap or lack that I had of family in my life. Not only have they filled the gaps, those areas of lack that were once in my heart, are now overflowing with love, blessing, affirmation, and encouragement - not just in my life, but in the lives of my children as well. For years, I was riddled with guilt because of the lack of grandparents in their lives. The gap in their lives that were so blatant and obvious, or so I thought. As the years passed, I began to see how God would fill the gap and make up for the lack in the hearts of my own children. This happened mostly through my in-laws, who are as wonderful as ten sets of grandparents. God has also filled their hearts through the precious people within our church family that have truly become family to me, my husband, and my children. THERE IS NO LACK IN OUR LIVES in any way.

Your family tree may not be big, beautiful, healthy, and whole, but it can be redeemed and restored. It may look a lot different than other people's, but it can become something that you can be proud of, even if it's only a trunk. ☺

# CHAPTER 22

## discussion questions

1. How would you describe your family tree?

2. Give your definition of dysfunction.

3. How has dysfunction infiltrated your family? Either immediate family or extended?

4. Read Matthew 1:1-6, 16 aloud. What hope does that bring your heart as you read those verses?

5. What are some of the truths that God revealed to you while reading this chapter?

6. How will your perspective change towards your family, both immediate and extended, after reading this chapter?

7. How has God made up for the lack in your life and the lives of those same family members?

8. Write out a prayer of gratitude for the grace of God you now realize that has been poured out over your life and the lives of your loved ones.

*conclusion*

# The Beauty of Spiritual Family

$\mathcal{A}llow$ me to give you some final thoughts on the very emotionally charged word: FAMILY.

Just the very word evokes a range of emotions: joy, happiness, love, endearment, fond memories, hurt, sadness, pain, loss, brokenness, heartache, regret, guilt, shame, gratitude, thankfulness, health, wellness, sacrifice, pride, security, faith, anger, fear, worry, doubt, togetherness, peace, loyalty, humility, and the list goes on and on.

Some of you have read this book and have found yourselves overwhelmed with gratitude for the wonderful family that raised you and surrounded you with their love. But probably for most of you, you have read this book and have related to the brokenness, the pain, and the wounds that I described within my own family growing up.

For those who find yourself in the latter category, please do not allow your upbringing and all that came with it, to disqualify you from all that God has planned for you and all of His purposes that He has laid out before you. Allow me and my story to be an example of God redeeming all that has been lost for His good and for His glory.

**There is great purpose on the other side of your greatest pain.**

You have to commit to push past that pain and allow God to heal your heart. Seek professional therapy and counseling if needed. Because on the other side of your healing, lies great peace and purpose. God can redeem the pain of your past too.

Psalm 68:5-6 says, *"A father to the fatherless (and a mother to the motherless...my addition☺), a defender of widows is God in His holy dwelling. God sets (places) the lonely in families..."*

Before the beginning of time, God already made a way and a place for you before you even came to the realization of how broken your family could be. It was never God's plan or intent for our earthly families to become so broken and fragmented. His intention was for us to live together in unity and togetherness, loving and respecting one another, caring for the needs of one another, and being an earthly representation to our world of what our Heavenly Father and His love for us looks like.

Sadly, in the majority of cases, that just isn't the way things turn out. We live in a fallen, sinful world where the brokenness and pain of sin has crept into our earthly families, and when that happens, brokenness and pain infiltrate our own hearts.

Our gracious God knew what sin would do to our families, and He created a "spiritual family" within the body of Christ, known as His church. When our earthly family fails us, our spiritual family will welcome us in. There is no perfect church, just as there is no perfect family. In areas where we are lacking in love, affirmation, acceptance, and forgiveness, our spiritual family, the church, can give us what our hearts so desperately need…a healthy family to become a part of.

If you are not a part of a church family, I urge you to find one.

Psalms 92:13-14 promises us: "…*those who are planted in the house of God will flourish in the courts of our God. They will still bear fruit in old age, they will stay fresh and green.*"

**You will begin to FLOURISH, GROW, and THRIVE as you plant yourself in the house of God. God will fill every lack you have in your earthly family with His spiritual family.**

Just as there are unhealthy families, there are unhealthy churches. Where pain and sorrow have infiltrated families, sadly that same pain and sorrow have infiltrated so many churches today. I promise you, there are healthy, vibrant churches out there. You just have to find them. Remember this: healthy things grow. Whether that's a marriage, a family, or a church, if it's healthy, it will grow. I am not necessarily speaking of how big the church is, I am speaking of how HEALTHY a church is. A healthy church has healthy leaders. A healthy church can be found.

Just as it would be unfair to judge every family against the pain that you have experienced in your own family, it would be equally unfair to judge a church against the pain you may have experienced in past church encounters. Ask God (and the wisdom of other healthy Christians) to lead and guide you as you search for the spiritual family that He desires to plant you in.

I honestly don't know where I would be today if not for my spiritual family. Within the house of God, I have found my healing, acceptance, affirmation, encouragement, forgiveness, and grace. I am not lacking in any way because of the loss of relationship with my earthly family. My spiritual family has become my FAMILY, and I will be forever grateful!

My heart and soul are healthy and whole because of God's healing touch on my life, and God so graciously leading me to His church, His house, and the people within it's walls…His family.

# CONCLUSION
## discussion questions

1. What are some of the emotions you experience when you hear the word "family"?

2. Concerning "family", what has been the greatest source of pain for you?

3. Have you been healed of that pain, or are you currently walking through your healing?

4. How has this book helped in your healing?

5. In your own words, describe what spiritual family means to you.

6. Are you currently joined to a healthy, vibrant, growing local church? If so, share that experience. If not, why? What steps do you need to take to find this kind of church family?

# ~final thoughts~

At the time of this writing, nothing in my earthly family has changed. There is still much that is broken. I do not know what the future holds for my family, but what I do know is this: God is good. He is faithful. He walks with me, and He has great plans and purposes for me. So in the meantime, I will carry on. I will continue to grow and love Him more. I will continue to guard my heart so that bitterness, resentment, and unforgiveness cannot creep back in. I will continue to share my story, so that prayerfully, my story can help others in their story, and I will continue to keep looking forward, not backward.

It has taken ten years for me to finally complete this book. Not because I am a slow writer, but because I was very broken. As I type these final thoughts, I can now see the delay in finishing this book has been God. Had I not taken the time and allowed God to complete the healing of my heart, I would have written this book from a wounded heart. Instead I write now from a healed heart, a whole heart, and a very grateful heart. The delay has been Divine. No question about it.

The wounds of my past and the hurt by my family are healed now. They are no longer open, gaping wounds but healed scars. The scars will never go away, as they serve as a reminder of the faithfulness and the forgiveness of my Redeemer, Jesus Christ. There is a hope for my future and the generations that come behind me.

**There is hope for you, too. There is healing, and there is wholeness for your broken, wounded heart.**
**Your Redeemer is there with you, and He, too, can find you in your field of brokenness.**

Just lift up your eyes to Him, lay at His feet, and ask Jesus to cover and redeem you. I promise you He will. He did for Ruth. He did for me, and He will do it for you, too.

My greatest purpose has been found within the place of my greatest pain. My greatest pain has been in my relationship with my mother or the lack of one. I have lived my whole life not knowing what a healthy relationship looks like with her. I can now see the gaping lack of emotional encouragement, support, and affirmation throughout my entire life. I know my mother did the very best she knew to do. I know my mother loved me, and had she known how to fix the brokenness in our relationship, she would have. I have no doubt about it.

As only God can do, He used my greatest pain to bring me to my greatest purpose: ministry to women. I have had the absolute privilege of standing before thousands of women across the country to speak God's heart and words to them and share the lessons of my own heart. I speak to the deepest places of a woman's heart because I know firsthand the pain that can reside there. I stand on stages, as a healed woman and mother, and speak to women in the audience as if they were my own daughters. I speak to them as if I were the one sitting and listening. My mindset is, " What would I have wanted someone to tell me thirty years ago? What encouragement could I have used? What words would have encouraged my heart and soothed my dry soul?", and then my message is an answer to those questions.

I have had the honor of standing beside my husband for over twenty-seven years and pastoring people. God's people. For the last fifteen years, we've had the privilege of helping pastor the precious people of Our Savior's Church in South Louisiana, and more recently, leading the campus in Opelousas, Louisiana. I've tried with all my heart to lead and pastor our women well through my words and my life example. I've seen with my own eyes how God heals the hearts of women as they bring their brokenness and pain to Him.

It takes time for God to heal your heart. It is a process and it doesn't happen overnight. The bigger the wounds, the longer the healing process, but healing can come. You have to be brutally honest with yourself first, then with God. You have to allow Him into the deepest, darkest, most painful places of your heart. You cannot walk away when you feel the pain. You must run to Him, your Redeemer, your

Healer, your Heavenly Father. You must fall at His feet and allow His presence to cover you, and you have to allow other healthy, Godly people to walk with you through your healing.

I know the pain of brokenness, but I also know the freedom and joy of wholeness. I will take the latter any day. God wastes nothing, not even your pain. Don't give up, and don't walk away. There are a lot of people needing your heart to be healed because they need to hear your story too. Your story of healing, your story of redemption, and your story of wholeness.

**Because on the other side of your greatest pain,**
**lies your greatest purpose.**

I am a living testament to that.

# acknowledgments

**Eugene:** My best friend, my greatest supporter, and my encourager! The healing of my heart and this book becoming a reality would NOT have happened without you! You refused to leave me to myself by lovingly leading me through this journey. You are truly the greatest gift that God has blessed me with! I love you!

**William:** You are a joy and gift to so many, especially ME. I am so proud of the man you have grown into, and I am so grateful that your dad and I have a front row seat to all that God has ahead of you! I love you!

**My Pastors, Jacob and Michelle Aranza:** Without a doubt, this book would not have happened without YOU. You have pastored me, spoken truth to me, laughed and cried with me, and believed in me, even when I did not believe in myself. Not only have you been our pastors, you have become our most treasured friends. Thank you for seeing something in me that I could not see. Thank you for the opportunities you have given me. I will never take that for granted. Thank you for giving Eugene and I a front row seat to all that God has done and continues to do through Our Savior's Church. We are humbled to be a part of something so divine! I love you both dearly!

**My Parents:** Thank you for giving your children a life you never had yourselves. I am so grateful. I pray that the same healing God has brought to my heart, has come to your hearts as well. I love you both.

**My In-Laws, Eugene Sr. and Nancy Reiszner:** You have accepted and loved me as your own daughter from day one. You will never know what that has meant to me! I love you both dearly and am so grateful God brought me into your family!

**The Women of Our Savior's Church:** You have walked with me through this journey of the book of Ruth for years. You have attended the Bible studies and listened to the messages, many times over! ☺ You have encouraged me, prayed for me, championed me, cried with me, and believed that I could write this book, even when I doubted it could ever happen. Yours were the faces on the other side of my computer screen every single day that I sat and poured out my heart. I will forever be grateful to you!

**My Childhood Pastors, Fred and Gloria Owens:** Thank you for loving and accepting me as part of your family so many years ago! You were the ones that taught me to love God's house and how to serve in building His kingdom. I will forever be indebted to you both. I would not be doing what I am doing today in ministry, had it not been for your investment in me! I love you very much!

**To the countless women who consider yourself my spiritual daughters, and even now, granddaughters (You know who you are ☺ ):** It has been my greatest joy to watch you grow, walk, and fulfill your God-given purposes! What you did not know was that as God used me to walk you through your healing, He was also healing my heart in the process. I am so proud of each of you!

**My Team of Editors:** Thank you for investing your time and expertise into this project. I am so thankful for your prayers, your input, and you cheering me on as we crossed the finish line in the completion of this book!

**To my Assistant, Donna:** Your tireless work and hours and hours of editing have not gone unnoticed. You were the one who made sure my heart was clearly represented within the pages of this book. There is not a doubt that the completion of this book happened because of your encouragement, your management of my schedule, and your help carrying the burden as we have crossed the finish line. Thank you!

**Our Savior's Church, Opelousas Campus and Staff:** Eugene and I are honored and privileged to serve as your pastors! We are humbled as you labor alongside of us. O-Town has been the greatest work and joy of our lives and we look ahead to the greatest days for Opelousas!

**Finally, Jesus, My Kinsman Redeemer:** Jesus, you have covered me, forgiven me, graced me, loved me, and redeemed me to a place of health and wholeness. I am humbled by the fact that you chose to use a once broken girl like me. I am forever grateful, as I lie at your feet, for the covering you continue to overshadow me with. I will spend the rest of my life bringing honor and glory to you, the One Who has redeemed and restored the broken areas of my once fragmented heart and soul.

# About the Author

Heidi Reiszner and her husband, Eugene, serve on the Executive Team of Our Savior's Church and its campuses. They are also the lead pastors of Our Savior's Church, Opelousas Campus – located in Opelousas, Louisiana. They have been married and in ministry for twenty-seven years. One of their greatest accomplishments has been raising three beautiful children: Hillary, Hannah, and William.

Heidi has led and equipped many to walking out this adventure called the "Christian Life" through teachings, blogs, missions, outreach and by the Godly example she gives to others. Heidi is passionate about Jesus and His kingdom. She finds delight in studying the Bible and teaching it. She helps others to understand His word in a simple way that is full of humor and truth. She loves building her community through various acts of love by making it a priority to give what she can for a city with so many needs. She also has a heart for world missions.

Through her ministry to women, Heidi equips women of all ages to become the person that God created them to be. Her nurturing spirit gives women of this generation something that is so desperately needed, a mother.

# contact information

If you enjoyed Redemption and would like more information or resources about Heidi Reiszner, please visit www.heidireiszner.com. On her website you will find Heidi's sermons, blogs, schedule, and contact information for speaking engagements.

You can also connect with Heidi through social media at:

Instagram: @heidireiszner
Facebook: www.facebook.com/heidireiszner
Twitter: @heidireiszner